TRIBALRY

— A BUSINESS TALE —

by Jared Stewart & Sarah Waugh

To all the official and unofficial editors inside our tribes whose feedback contributed so greatly to the writing and publishing of this book.

TABLE OF CONTENTS

1.

Harry Green

You never miss the water until the well has run dry.

—Irish Proverb

Harry sat up, gasping for air. His sweat-soaked shirt was clinging to his skin, and the rapid pounding of his heart echoed loudly in his ears.

It was just a dream, he told himself, recognizing the familiar shapes of his darkened bedroom. He looked over the shoulder of his sleeping wife at the clock sitting on her nightstand. The glowing numbers read 12:07 a.m.

Rolling over, he tried to force himself back to sleep, but it was no use. He pushed back the blanket and made his way down the stairs.

As Harry walked through the quiet house, the violent images of his nightmare began replaying in his mind. For three straight months he'd been alternating between insomnia and night terrors, and it was getting worse. Harry's family had always teased him about being a hypochondriac, but this time he was certain something was really wrong.

At the end of the hallway, Harry saw that the lamp in his office was still on. He'd been spending so much time away from his family that he'd recently added an office to his home. Sitting at his desk, Harry moved aside a tray stacked high with financial reports and legal documents and switched on his computer. When he opened his inbox, his heart sank. Twenty-nine new emails. Harry had just finished a book on positive thinking, but he was willing to bet that none of the emails contained good news.

As he scanned through the subject lines, he spotted one with his teenage nickname, "Green Machine," and opened it. The message was from his best friend, asking when they could get together for lunch. Harry realized that it had been almost six months since he'd seen Mark. They'd been inseparable in high school and stayed close ever since, but Harry couldn't seem to find time for anyone these days.

He closed that email and noticed another, flagged as urgent. The subject line read "Tomorrow's Battle." With a puzzled frown, Harry opened the message and read its contents:

Gladiator,

It is only by the intervention of the gods that you live to see another dawn.

Your cowardly performance on the field of battle continues to provide little drama for my crowds, but as long as your heart still beats inside your chest, I am obligated to schedule your next match.

Please arrive early.

Sincerely,

Victor Sludge

Director of Coliseum Events

Harry stared at the monitor, his mouth hanging open in disbelief. Was it possible that his nightmares had found a way to torment his waking hours as well? Suddenly the screen snapped shut, replaced by an error notification. Harry reopened his mailbox and searched through the messages, but the email had disappeared.

Maybe my brain is still asleep he thought, trying to stifle the panic rising in his chest. In an effort to distract himself, Harry began organizing his desk. He gathered stray pens and highlighters and put them into a cup beside the computer, then began separating the overdue bills from his banking statements and tax returns. Beneath the clutter, he uncovered a packet of information and read the large yellow sticky attached to it:

Harry,

Here are the financial reports I promised. Sorry, but it looks like we're going to be short again this week. Losing the Strickland account took its toll. I'll put the other payments on hold, but if we're going to make payroll, I'll need an additional $30,000 by Friday.

Dan

In a small fit of rage, Harry jerked open the middle drawer and swept the papers in.

Out of sight, out of mind. He was about to slam the drawer shut when he spotted the corner of a leather-bound book peeking out from underneath the stack of papers. *That's where you went.*

The book was the early journal of Patrick O'Flannery, the business partner of Harry's great-great-grandfather George Green. Despite impossible odds, George and Patrick had become two of New York's most influential industrialists, and their rags-to-riches story had always fascinated Harry.

All that was known about George's early life was that he'd left the family farm for New York City when he was about fifteen years old. Even less had been known about Patrick's background—until now. The brittle paper and smudged ink of the recently discovered journal provided a detailed account of how Patrick and his family had narrowly escaped starvation during the Irish Potato Famine, joining the throng of immigrants that had flocked to the United States during the 1840s.

Harry had devoured the journal's contents in just a few sittings, but to his frustration, the account had ended with Patrick's arrival in America. It didn't cover the period when Patrick had met George or given any clues as to how they had been able to achieve their legendary success.

What would they have done in my place? Harry asked himself as he absently leafed through the journal's yellowing pages.

He thought back to how confident he'd been when he'd started out. At twenty-one, he'd applied for his first real job—one way out of his league—and the CEO had made the controversial decision to give the cocky kid a shot. Although Harry was the youngest member of the team and the only person without extensive industry experience, it never bothered him. He planned on outworking his coworkers and out-thinking his competition. With determined effort and an iron will, he became the team's top producer and a rising star within the company. Then, about a year later, the entrepreneurial bug bit hard.

It started the day Harry invited his friend Jackson Miller to lunch. They discovered they both hoped to go into business for themselves someday, and by the end of their fifth sushi roll, they had the beginnings of a business plan. Using their middle names, they called the company Dillon-Parker and felt certain they were about to revolutionize the world of brand management. Because of his background and business experience, Harry was given the role of CEO. It would be his job to lead the company to success.

I walked out of there on cloud nine, Harry remembered.

It was a risky move, but Harry was impulsive and determined to succeed. After all, he was the youngest and most successful member of his team. Why not take his talents to the next level? Working from his home, he netted over $30,000 his first month. Emboldened by his success, he secured a loan, signed a lease, and started hiring the best people he could find, starting with Jackson Miller. Within eighteen months, Dillon-Parker was one of the top five branding companies in the region.

Harry remembered the exhilaration he'd experienced as they'd pinpointed the perfect spot to build their new offices. His good friend Vince Matthews had pulled a few strings at Oak Grove Community Bank to secure the financing. Harry had convinced six of his colleagues to leave their current jobs and join his new management team. But his biggest accomplishment had been selling his security-loving wife on the idea. He'd been on fire, completely unstoppable.

Images of Dillon-Parker's grand opening flashed through Harry's mind. He vividly remembered his staff surrounding him as he cut the ribbon, raising their glasses to toast the arrival of the world's greatest force in advertising.

I worked my butt off and often outproduced the rest of my team combined, Harry thought.

Half the time it felt like his team just sat around and watched him work, which bothered him, but he didn't have time to do anything about it. Someone had to keep this thing growing, and if necessary, he would do it alone. He'd beaten down his vendors to get the lowest prices and had assumed every "no" just meant "not yet." Sure, he'd made some enemies along the way, but Harry had always prided himself on being a business pragmatist, patterning his life after his favorite quote in *The Godfather*, "It's not personal, it's just business."

And we were doing just fine . . . until they let the tigers out.

While Harry had been focusing on the battle in front of him, something deadly had attacked from behind. Dillon-Parker had launched their business at the height of a boom market. The first twelve months had been nirvana; the second twelve, slow torture. Eight of their top ten clients went out of business or decided to significantly reduce the amount of money they were spending on their brands. It took only ten months to burn through their entire two-million-dollar line of credit. After that was gone, Harry began liquidating his personal assets: first his real estate investments, then his stocks, and finally he had taken every penny of equity out of their home.

Now, four years later, the company was still losing money. Harry tried to trim costs where he could, but it seemed like every other week he was scrambling to make payroll. His overhead was crushing him, and his team still wasn't producing. The most talented half had given up and moved on to other opportunities, and the staff that remained just seemed to be waiting out the inevitable.

I've completely ruined my life. What was I thinking?

Earlier that week, he'd received a call from an attorney informing him that a major client had just declared bankruptcy and wasn't planning on paying their $75,000 invoice. In desperation, Harry had spent significant time the last couple of days following up on a major lead—Will Clay, from Clay & Chagall. At this point, landing a huge account like theirs might be the only way to save the company—but so far they'd only gotten radio silence. Despite giving it every ounce of strength and courage he possessed, Harry's company was slowly bleeding to death.

His dream had officially turned into a nightmare.

It should be working! What am I leaving out? Harry slammed the palm of his hand on the desk, oblivious to the resulting sting. "Will someone please tell me what I'm missing?" he asked aloud.

Half expecting an answer, he sat in silence for a few minutes. Then, with a sigh, he tucked the journal under his arm and headed for the kitchen. Lately, eating was the only thing that eased his pain.

He opened the refrigerator door and rummaged around, finally emerging with a few red-chili burritos and a quart of chocolate peanut butter ice cream. While waiting for the burritos to heat up, he took out a mixing bowl and started scooping ice cream into it. As he moved around the kitchen, he found it painful to look at the granite countertops and steel appliances. He and his wife had purchased their new home with the assumption of prosperity; he'd never contemplated the possibility of failure. When he thought of the current state of his business—and the prospect of losing everything he'd worked so hard for—the knot in the pit of his stomach tightened, and he found it difficult to breathe.

Mercifully, the microwave buzzer interrupted his thoughts, and Harry began loading his arms with food. Going into the den, he settled himself into his favorite chair. As Harry set the bowl of ice cream on a side table, he saw a picture book and felt a stab of guilt. He'd arrived home that evening to discover his youngest daughter asleep on his chair, the book clutched in her tiny hands. His wife explained that she'd insisted on waiting up for the bedtime story he'd promised to read her. The brightly illustrated pigs on the cover were a painful reminder that Harry was failing at much more than just his business.

In a desperate attempt to distract his mind, Harry reached for the remote. In the past he'd avoided television, feeling his time was better spent working toward his goals.

And look where that's gotten me.

2.
Patrick O'Flannery

It is difficult to put a wise head on young shoulders.
—Irish Proverb

As Harry flipped through the channels, he came across a black-and-white film version of *A Christmas Carol*. It seemed an odd programming choice for mid-September, but he figured it was better than an infomercial and settled in to watch.

Jacob Marley had just appeared to warn Scrooge of the fate that awaited him as a consequence of his miserly ways. His clanking chains provided a chilling visual aid to his words. The eeriness of the scene brought Harry's nightmares back to the forefront of his mind.

On the screen, a terrified Scrooge protested, "But you were always a good man of business, Jacob."

"Business!" cried the ghost. "Mankind was my business. The common welfare was my business. The dealings of my trade were but a drop of water in the comprehensive ocean of my business."

A sense of impending doom swept through Harry, but he found himself unable to take his eyes from the screen.

Jacob Marley seemed to be speaking directly to him. "I am here tonight to warn you that you have a chance of escaping my fate. You will be haunted by spirits tonight, and without their visits you cannot hope to shun the path I tread."

The stillness of the room seemed to intensify. It was as if everything around him was poised, waiting for something to happen.

Suddenly a voice from behind Harry called out, "Good evenin' to you, lad!"

Harry leapt from his chair and turned to face the intruder. To his amazement, he saw a man sitting on his leather couch, eating popcorn from a large plastic bowl. Wisps of hair peeked out from underneath his cap, and a bag of golf clubs lay at his feet, the bag's exterior embroidered with a shamrock insignia.

Speaking in an Irish brogue, the man continued. "You'll be excusing me not doing my own introduction, but 'tis terrible difficult to compete with Jacob Marley. Since he retired, the foundation's had quite a time finding an adequate replacement."

The man reached into his golf bag and pulled out a small computer.

"What?" Harry finally choked out.

"I've been assigned as your trainer," the man explained pleasantly. "Your call came in at . . ." He flipped open a laptop, his fingers moving like lightning across the keys. "12:29 a.m." He checked his watch with a furrowed brow. "We have a ten-minute guaranteed arrival time, and I'm a wee bit late. But I'm hoping you'll be kind enough to overlook that, seeing as how the call was made outside normal business hours."

"There must be some mistake," Harry mumbled, rubbing his eyes.

"No mistake. The fee was electronically charged to your credit card." The stranger's fingers raced over the keys again. "The number was 9876 . . . saints above!" The man exclaimed in sudden comprehension. "A foundation account."

Seeing the bewildered look on Harry's face, the man quickly explained. "Forgive me, lad. I was in such a state getting here that I only glanced over your file. Let's see if I can explain." He rubbed his chin reflectively. "You see, the foundation I work for sometimes takes special cases pro bono when they feel the need is great and the potential high. You must've qualified on both counts."

The man stopped and leaned forward slightly, examining Harry with a puzzled expression. "Have we met? You do be putting me in mind of someone."

He pulled out a manila folder from the golf bag, and Harry could see a sheaf of papers with his photograph clipped to the top. The man scanned through the pages, then suddenly his head snapped up, and he stared at Harry in astonishment.

"Glory be! 'Tis a wonder I didn't be seeing the family resemblance right off." His eyes twinkled as he stretched out his hand to shake Harry's. "I don't believe we've been properly introduced. Patrick O'Flannery, at your service."

"Oh, I get it," Harry said with a wave of relief. "I'm still dreaming."

"A common response," Patrick replied, nodding. "That's what Scrooge thought as well. He was another pro-bono case, and although it was considered a bit of a risk at the time, the whole thing ended quite brilliantly. It's cited fourteen times in the handbook, you know."

Harry didn't respond but dug his fingernails into his palms, trying to create enough pain to wake himself up.

"What a grand joke, sending me to you without a warning word!" Patrick continued, slapping his palm against his knee. "But it's delighted I am to be here all the same. I owe a great debt to George Green—one I'll never be able to fully repay, but it appears as if I'm to be given the chance to try."

"But you can't be Patrick O'Flannery. You died over a hundred years ago!" Harry exclaimed. It seemed pointless to argue with someone who didn't exist, but he couldn't help himself.

"Now then, I can't be explaining all the ins and outs of life and death. You'll just have to be trusting that I am who I say." Patrick stopped short as he caught sight of the journal on the table. "Ah! Now there's a sight that brings back memories."

Harry reached out and picked up the journal.

"I've been reading it for the past couple of days," he told Patrick. "To tell you the truth, I haven't been able to put it down."

Patrick took the book from Harry, gently rubbing its cracked leather binding as he spoke. "Aye, you would be relating to this part of me story. You're in the middle of your own kind of famine, aren't you? That's why I'm here."

"Yeah, it looks like they pulled you out of a pretty important appointment," Harry said with a trace of amusement, observing Patrick's striped shirt and khakis.

"Now, Harry Green, that kind of thinking right there is the root of your problem," Patrick replied. "Why do you be supposing so many business students take golfing lessons? Do you have the least notion how much business takes place over a nine iron? Mergers, partnerships, securing big accounts—they've all been cemented over a wee ball and heaps of grass."

Then, as though he were imparting a great secret, Patrick leaned in and said, "I'll risk a wager that you be one of those lads who think that success is about numbers and transactions. But success is about relationships."

Harry looked at him incredulously. "Let me get this straight. My great-great-grandfather's business partner came back from the dead to tell me that the answer to my problems is playing more golf?"

Patrick threw his hands up in exasperation. "Do you be having some problems with your hearin', Harry Green?" he asked. "Because you don't seem to be listenin'. I didn't say success is about golf. I said, success is about *relationships*."

A tinkling rendition of "Danny Boy" rang out, and Harry jumped as though he'd been bitten. The sound seemed to come from the golf bag at Patrick's feet.

"My apologies, lad!" Flustered, Patrick quickly dove into his golf bag and turned off the phone. "Turning off the phone is rule number one in the Code of Conduct."

Harry stood up and headed for the bathroom.

"Where are you off to? We'll be hard set to finish by morning as it is," Patrick called after him.

"To get some medication," Harry called over his shoulder. "I'm so sleep deprived I've gone delusional. I am hallucinating a four-foot, Irish Bobby Jones."

Patrick raised himself up to his full height. "I'm well over five feet."

Harry ignored him. "Or maybe I've finally fallen asleep and you're my brain's twisted version of *It's a Wonderful Life.*"

"One of me favorite movies!" Patrick said, his eyes shining. When Harry didn't respond, Patrick called after him. "Heed this, lad. I'm not a dream, and you shouldn't be so surprised, seeing as I'm here per your request."

"What request? I didn't ask you for anything," Harry called out as he unscrewed the lid of a small prescription bottle.

"Beggin' your pardon, but you did." Patrick typed furiously on his laptop. "At exactly 12:29 a.m., you said, 'Will someone please tell me what I'm missing?'"

Two pills slipped from Harry's grip and clattered onto the tile floor. He stepped out of the bathroom, his eyes wide with surprise.

Patrick continued. "But if you don't be wanting me services after all, I'll be goin'. I was in the middle of the game of me life, you know."

"Look," Harry finally said, "as nice as it is to meet you, I'm at a point where I can't afford to waste any more energy on something that isn't going to work."

"Be'gorah, lad!" Patrick exclaimed. "You could give a mule lessons in stubbornness! What other choice do you have? You've tried everythin' you can think of and have come up all sixes and sevens. So, I'll be askin' you once more, Harry Green, will you be wanting to know what you're missin' or not?"

For the first time, Harry entertained the possibility that this might really be happening. He slowly ran his fingers through his hair, trying to forecast the possible consequences of accepting Patrick's offer.

"My life is coming apart at the seams. If things don't change soon, I'll lose everything," Harry admitted. He paused for a minute, then finished reluctantly. "Yes, I want to know. What will I have to do?"

"Well, first off, I'll be needin' a little participation. Like the saying goes, 'Neither give cherries to pigs nor advice to a fool,'" Patrick said.

Harry sighed. "Well, like you said, I've got nothing to lose."

As he spoke these words, the grandfather clock in the hallway struck one. The gong was louder and longer than normal and increased in volume until it was deafening. Harry put his hands over his ears and squeezed his eyes shut.

3.
The Gladiator

A man may be his own ruin.

—Irish Proverb

Harry felt the pressure of a dense crowd around him, and when he opened his eyes, he found himself surrounded by thousands of people. He didn't understand the language they spoke, but judging from the way they were dressed, it appeared as though he'd been transported to ancient Rome. Harry noticed that his pajamas and slippers had been replaced with a toga and leather sandals, and Patrick was nowhere in sight.

Desperately searching the crowd, he spotted Patrick and pushed toward him. As soon as he was close enough, Harry grabbed his trainer's arm.

"This is going too far, even for one of my psychotic dreams," he said through clenched teeth. "Where am I?"

Instead of answering Harry's question, Patrick held up two leather squares, each stamped with an intricate design.

"'Tis your lucky day, lad. I just happen to have two tickets for the senators' pavilion," he said.

A blast of trumpets sounded, and the crowd began lumbering forward, the mass of bodies sweeping Harry and Patrick toward the entrance of an enormous coliseum.

After passing underneath two massive archways, the interior of the coliseum came into view. Harry's jaw dropped in astonishment as he saw tens of thousands of people slowly filling the stone risers.

"We'd best be finding our seats," Patrick said, nudging him forward.

Navigating a labyrinth of stone stairways, they eventually arrived inside an enclosed balcony overlooking the arena. Harry's eyes were immediately drawn to a bright silk awning that shielded a table filled with appetizing dishes.

"I think you'll enjoy a bit of the shrimp and melons, and even the fish soufflé," Patrick said as they picked up their plates. He gestured to a dish near the end of the table and added, "But I'd steer clear of that one."

"Why?" Harry asked, leaning forward to examine the dish. "What is it?"

"Peacock tongues," Patrick replied, grinning at Harry's disgusted expression. "They're not bad with a pinch of cinnamon, but I still don't think you'd fancy them."

They took their seats, and after successfully balancing his heaping plate on his lap, Harry looked out over the playing field for the first time. Formidable fifteen-foot walls surrounded it; large boulders and wooden structures dotted the field of play. A wave of recognition broke over him, followed by a second wave of nausea.

"I can't stay here," he gasped, spilling his food on the stone floor as he rose to his feet.

"Steady there, lad," Patrick said, laying a hand on his arm. "Why don't you just take a breath and tell me what's wrong."

Cold fear began pulsing through Harry's veins. "You don't understand. I've fought a thousand battles on that field. That place is my nightmare!"

Patrick nodded. "Right, I know all about your dreams, lad. That's the reason I brought you here—to empty the box so we can fill it again."

Their conversation was interrupted by the sound of screeching metal against stone. Inside the arena two chains spun into motion, lifting an iron gate until it locked into place. The trumpets sounded as a lone figure passed through the gate.

Watching in horrified fascination, Harry sank back into his seat. He knew the dank smell of the tunnel the gladiator had just exited and could almost feel the weight of the armor on his chest and shoulders. He was looking at himself.

The gladiator placed a helmet on his head, shifting it back and forth until it slipped into place. Then, after selecting a shield and sword from the stockpile of weapons, he climbed the raised platform at the center of the arena. He raised his sword high in the air, and the crowd responded with a deafening roar.

Without warning, the doors on the east and west sides of the arena heaved open, and two armored chariots appeared, each driven by a different gladiator. Another loud cheer exploded from the crowd. One of these gladiators, arrayed in blue and gray, skillfully guided his team of horses into position. With a flick of his whip, the huge animals lunged forward and quickly gained speed as they raced across the arena toward the lone gladiator.

"I can't do this again," Harry muttered under his breath.

"Better to watch him than to stand in his place," Patrick whispered back.

Harry looked at Patrick incredulously. "Is that supposed to make me feel better?"

Harry turned back to see his gladiator-self dive out of the way, dust billowing around him as he slammed into the ground. His opponent wheeled his chariot around and headed toward him. This time he struck a blow with his trident, ripping off Harry's breastplate and tearing cruelly into the flesh underneath. Back in the pavilion, Harry clutched his side, almost expecting to have felt the blow, but his eyes never left the field.

Staggering toward a great stone monolith at the edge of the arena, Harry saw himself hide behind it as the other two gladiators engaged in battle. Their exchange was brief, and within minutes the same gladiator who had injured Harry raised his bloody sword in victory.

As the crowd chanted its approval, the victorious charioteer wheeled his horses around and drew out a large spear.

"He's going to kill me, isn't he?" Harry groaned.

As the gladiator rumbled near, Harry watched himself feint left and jump onto the back of the chariot. Then, using all his weight, he dragged his opponent from the chariot and onto the ground. Taking a step backward, he unsheathed a dagger and plunged it into his enemy. The crowd cheered wildly as the opposing gladiator slumped to the ground. Red and white rose petals filled the air, slowly fluttering to the arena floor.

Looking around at the chanting crowd, Harry blurted out, "What are they saying? After every battle they chant the same words."

"*Habet, hoc habet*," Patrick explained. "It means 'He has had it.'"

Harry watched himself salute the crowd, then collapse. Two slaves came onto the field and carried him away, leaving a dark trail of blood behind them.

"Am I going to be all right?" Harry asked.

"Will you listen to that," Patrick said as the crowd continued to cheer wildly. He seemed unaware that Harry had asked a question. "The whole lot of them on their feet hailing you as a hero. This is quite the dream you've been having."

"It's not a dream; it's a nightmare. I've been coming here nearly every night for three weeks. Sometimes I win, but more often I . . ." Harry's voice trailed off. "Needless to say, I don't look forward to going to sleep anymore."

Patrick nodded sympathetically. Then, glancing down at his watch, he gave a start. "Spells and curses, would you look at the time! Are you ready, then?"

"For what?" Harry asked, looking around apprehensively.

"For the alternative to the coliseum."

Fire Triangle

4.

The Fire Triangle

There is not strength without unity.

—Irish Proverb

The coliseum was suddenly swallowed up in darkness. When Harry opened his eyes he found himself lying flat on his back, staring up at a cloud-filled sky. A salty ocean breeze danced on his lips, and he heard the pounding of the surf in the distance.

Standing up, he found himself on a dirt pathway that wound itself toward a tropical village, its grass huts tucked in between lush trees and flowering bushes. The path continued past the village and ended at a white sandy beach and turquoise bay.

"Greetings!"

Harry whirled around to see a large Polynesian man wearing a lavalava. On his bare chest hung several strands of brown wooden beads, partially obscuring an intricate tribal tattoo beneath.

"Where am I?" Harry asked.

The man let out a long laugh and in a resonant bass voice proclaimed, "A better question is when are you? Welcome to 200 BC, the golden age of tribes. I am Afu, leader of my people."

The man's features radiated integrity and genuine care. Harry could easily see why the villagers had chosen him to be their leader.

"Patrick has asked that I prepare you to learn the secrets of tribalry."

"Is that some kind of primitive carpentry?" Harry asked dubiously. "Because I'm not very handy—just ask my wife."

Afu just shook his head and continued "Tribalry is the ancient art of building connection and community. When the three elements of tribalry are combined, they unlock the power of the fire triangle and turn your dreams into realities. Come, I will show you."

Harry followed Afu down the pathway into the center of the village. He motioned for Harry to sit on one of the circular rocks that surrounded a large fire pit and sat directly across from him.

"How did you enjoy the sport of the coliseum?" Afu asked, his white grin flashing.

"I would rather have eaten the peacock tongues and skipped the main attraction," Harry replied. "You guys certainly don't pull any punches when trying to make a point."

"True. Perhaps the foundation has had too much time to 'improve' upon the training," Afu suggested with a chuckle. "Regardless, the coliseum teaches its lesson well. I have never forgotten my time there and I am happy to never see that deadly place again."

"How did you get out? I don't want to go back—ever," Harry blurted out almost involuntarily.

Afu looked at Harry with deep sympathy. "In truth, you have been living the life of a gladiator by day and by night. In one arena you wear a breastplate and carry a sword, and in the other you wear a business suit and carry a computer."

Afu's gaze seemed to pierce right through him.

"Gladiators symbolize the part of our nature that wants to conquer alone. Instead of building trusted relationships, Gladiators see others as opponents or obstacles. Their viewpoint is always competitive: If others win, they lose. For them, life is a jungle with only two choices: become the predator or become the prey. Does that sound right?"

"A little melodramatic, but I guess it's accurate," Harry admitted reluctantly. "But that's just business, right?"

"Yes, gladiators do wield tremendous influence in your day and the very best fighters are heralded as heroes—and who doesn't want to be a hero?" Afu asked. "But don't be fooled. The coliseum is a very dangerous place, and no one survives in there forever."

Afu picked up a stick from the dirt and sifted through the ashes of the fire pit as he continued, "Harry, you are a modern player in an ancient game. The sad truth is, when your business dies on the field of battle—and it will die—your gladiator friends will simply write off their losses and move along to the next contender."

Afu turned and looked directly into Harry's eyes, "I understand that the coliseum has its benefits. The roar of the crowd, the chanting of your name . . .you can't help but want more and more of it. But like any addiction, it also has a cost. While you've been inside the coliseum feeding your ego, your business has lost half its top talent, antagonized its key vendors, and alienated the majority of your customer base. Your tribe is, what do you call it, a village of spirits?"

"A ghost town," Harry absently corrected him.

Harry had the same impression the night before as he walked the empty halls of Dillon-Parker. Each office felt like a silo, where the occupants lived separate lives, disconnected from everyone else as well as from the company's mission. They were going through the motions, but Afu was right—they had mentally checked out. Afu's brutal assessment of his vendor and customer relationships was also painfully accurate.

"Agreed," said Harry resolutely. "But what's the alternative?"

"There is only one path that leads away from the coliseum," Afu said soberly. "You must shun the ways of a gladiator and build a tribe instead."

"A tribe?" Harry said, looking around at the grass huts with raised eyebrows. "I think you better recalibrate that time machine of yours. In my time, we don't live in tribes."

"You are wrong, Harry Green," Afu said earnestly. "Tribes are, and will always be, the heartbeat of every people. They are the tide on which each nation rises and falls." Afu gestured to the pocket that held Harry's mobile phone. "Let's use some of the magic from your day. Kindly search the word 'tribes.'"

Harry pulled out his phone and was surprised to find it had a signal. He performed the search and read the results aloud.

> *1. A community of people who have similar values or interests, a shared ancestor or common leader, and who live in a face-to-face setting and are bound by kinship ties, reciprocal exchanges, and strong ties to a place.*

> *2. A company, group, or set of persons with shared characteristics, occupations, or interests.*

"Based on that definition," Afu said, "can you think of any tribes that exist in your day?"

Harry pondered this for a moment, then began ticking off examples on his fingers: his work tribe, church tribe, neighborhood tribe, his best friend Mark's animal rescue tribe, and his sister's homeschooling tribe. Harry lifted his eyebrows in surprise at how easy it had been. The world suddenly teemed with tribes.

"This is good," Afu said approvingly.

Harry was on a roll. "Wait, there's more. My brother's basketball tribe, my business school tribe and, most importantly, my family tribe."

"You were blind but now you see," Afu proclaimed. "Now that you can see the world of tribes, it is time to let fire be your teacher. Tell me, what are the three things fire needs to start and survive?"

After a moment of thought, Harry responded, "Well, something to burn. Fuel."

Afu handed Harry a primitive looking bamboo shovel. Working together, they cleared out the ashes of the fire pit and then began gathering twigs and dry palm fronds, and Afu molded the materials into a small tinder brick.

"What else?" Afu prompted.

"Heat. Something to ignite it," Harry replied. "A match or anything that creates a spark."

Afu picked up two stones near the pit and expertly struck one against the other to produce a shower of sparks that fell like a waterfall onto the tinder.

Seeing Harry's expression, Afu shrugged his shoulders and grinned. "I think perhaps we are defter with our hands than those of your generation."

Some of the sparks had nested themselves inside the tinder and were glowing like red jewels.

Afu continued, "These sparks will die without the final element."

"Oxygen."

Afu nodded his encouragement and Harry crouched down on a woven mat of palm leaves near the fire to blow gently on the embers. One ignited and greedily ate the tinder, then blossomed into a licking mass of yellow-and-orange flame.

"Well done," Afu said, slapping Harry on the back. "For a man of technology."

They continued to fuel the fire with larger and larger branches until it was well established. Harry smiled, enjoying the glow of the flames, but as the larger logs began their slow burn to ashes, he became melancholy. How was any of this supposed to help him?

"Fire is the power that gives life to my tribe," Afu responded, as if reading Harry's thoughts. "It gives us light in the darkness, heat for the cold, and warmth to our food. Tribes in your day are powered by the same three elements."

Harry raised an eyebrow. "Fire 2.0?"

"Right, just as this fire needs each element to perform its function, all successful tribes—whether they be work tribes, family tribes, club tribes, or any other brand of tribe—all need fuel, heat, and oxygen to ignite and thrive."

Afu handed Harry a golden triangle with a flame carved into its center and told Harry that at the striking of each hour, a different trainer would appear to instruct him on the principles and practices that combined to create each arm of the fire triangle—the three elements of tribalry.

"It seems our time is done," Afu said, as he swept a hand up to where the sun had begun its descent below the horizon. "Good luck, my friend. Mahalo."

TRIBE5

Decide to Tribe

Invisible Threads

Avoid Relationship Arrogance

Just Because

Learn, Serve, Grow

PrinCiPLeS
(FUeL)

5.
Decide To Tribe

As the old cock crows, the young cock learns.

—Irish Proverb

As Afu's face began to blur, Harry blinked his eyes, trying to clear his vision, his surroundings fading into blackness. When he heard the familiar chimes of his hallway clock, he exhaled deeply; he was home. He heard a quiet click, and the room became illuminated. Turning around, Harry saw Patrick sitting in his leather armchair, the lamp softly bathing him in light.

"What else can I do?" Harry asked, at a total loss. "I work an insane number of hours every week, and I've contributed every financial resource I have, not to mention my physical and emotional health. If this business has any success, it's due to my efforts, and if it fails, it's because no one else has the same level of commitment. Without me this company wouldn't have had a snowball's chance in hell."

Patrick knelt beside him and spoke quietly. "Right, you've fought match after match, and you've the battle scars to prove it. No one has worked harder, fought smarter, or sacrificed more than you." Patrick gently laid a hand on Harry's arm. "I'm not sayin' you haven't done everythin' you can, lad. What I'm sayin' is, it's just not enough."

"Oh, it's comforting to know that *everything* isn't enough," Harry retorted.

"You're treadin' the path of a gladiator and are bound to its inevitable end," Patrick said, returning to the seat across from Harry. "Perhaps the time has come for me to be sharin' a bit more about me life in Ireland. 'Tis not a time I care to be rememberin', but it may help you to hear it."

Harry tried to hold on to his anger, but he felt it draining away as Patrick told his story. His words, lilting with the accent of his native country, captivated Harry as completely as the journal had.

Lightly touching on how he had met his wife, Molly, and on the happy arrival of their two sons, Patrick moved on to describe how their lives had taken a sharp turn for the worse during the bleak years of the potato famine. By the second year of the famine, Patrick and

Molly routinely set out at daybreak to search the barren fields, sifting through the dirt in search of something edible. Each night they returned to their sons with barely enough to avoid starvation.

Patrick's voice grew husky as he described watching his children become more and more emaciated. He finally fell silent as Patrick seemed to be reliving some private scene.

"You and I aren't so different, lad," he finally said. "I started workin' me land with great dreams for the future. When lean times came, I met the challenge the only way I knew how, as a gladiator waging my own private battle with fate. Year after year, I kept plantin' potatoes that came up rotten. In the end, I had to be choosing between certain death or changin' me path." He sat silently for several moments before concluding, "History does have a way of repeatin' itself. You, Harry Green, now find yourself at the same crossroad. You can either hold to the path of a gladiator, continuin' to answer the summons of the coliseum until you die on the battlefield, or you can be choosin' a different path."

"By becoming a tribe leader?" Harry asked.

Patrick nodded. "Do you have the fire triangle Afu gave you?" he asked.

Harry pulled the small golden triangle from his pocket and held it in his hand. Suddenly the base of the triangle ignited, and the word "Principles" appeared.

"Just like fuel is the foundation of a fire, principles are the foundation of any endeavor in life or business. But all fuel isn't of equal worth. Paper can start a fire but can't support it over time like wood can. In the same way, strong principles—the right kind of fuel—are the key to creatin' healthy relationships. The first arm of tribalry is a specific set of principles that, if followed, will help tribe relationships grow and prosper. These key principles are called the Tribe5."

"Sounds like a boy band my daughter might like," Harry muttered under his breath.

Patrick gave him a pointed look and continued.

"The first Tribe5 principle is all about the tribe leader. Tell me this: What one thing does every great tribe leader have in common?"

Answering Patrick's question was more difficult than Harry expected. Tribe leaders were male and female, old and young, rich and poor, charismatic and reserved. They led all kinds of different tribes—families, congregations, companies, friends, and teams. What trait did leaders of these diverse groups all share? In the end, he just shrugged his shoulders and held up his hands.

"Perhaps another story will help. 'Tis about a famous Scottish climber named William Hutchison Murray. While a prisoner of war during WWII, Mr. Murray wrote an entire mountaineering book using only scraps of toilet paper. When the Gestapo discovered the book, it was quickly destroyed. But William was a determined soul and simply started again. Even though the prison conditions made it doubtful he'd live, he continued to write."

"That would take a lot of faith," Harry said, impressed. "Did he climb again?

"Aye, lad. He was part of several expeditions, and his books created a post-WWII renaissance inside the sport."

From his bag, Patrick drew out a card with an image of a smoky mountain peak on the back and a W. H. Murray quote across the front.

> Until one is committed, there is hesitancy, the chance to draw back, always ineffectiveness. Concerning all acts of initiative (and creation), there is one elementary truth, the ignorance of which kills countless ideas and splendid plans: that the moment one definitely commits oneself, then Providence moves too... A whole stream of events issues from the decision, raising in one's favour all manner of unforeseen incidents and meetings and material assistance, which no man could have dreamt would have come his way.

Harry stood staring silently at the card, the words still ringing in his ears.

"All tribe leaders share this defining moment—the moment they irrevocably commit themselves to building a tribe and embrace the responsibility of being its fearless leader," Patrick said. "You've shown the grit to fight for your company, the question is whether you can muster the same amount of commitment to build a tribe."

"That's the first principle?"

"Decide to tribe," Patrick affirmed. "But leading a tribe is no small decision. It takes courage to blaze new trails in the wilderness."

Patrick rummaged through his golf bag and emerged with a document printed in dark green ink and bearing the official seal of the foundation.

"With that said, we cannot go any further without the necessary documentation and signatures. I can ill afford to mix it up with legal again," Patrick said as he handed the document to Harry. "Take your time and read it carefully, lad."

When Harry finished reading, Patrick pointed to the final line and asked, "Will you please read this last bit aloud?"

Harry cleared his throat. "'I hereby agree to suspend judgment and to complete all aspects of the training in full.'"

He looked at Patrick questioningly.

"I'm happy to lend a hand, but I don't waste my time with fence-sitters. If you're not ready to pledge yourself to complete the trainin', then we best say our good-byes now. If you sign the agreement, you will be seeing this through to the end.

The faces of Harry's family, partners, and employees played through his mind. He picked up the pen and slowly signed his name.

6.
Invisible Threads

Pity him who makes his opinions a certainty.
—Irish Proverb

The next thing Harry was aware of was feeling a cold, smooth, solid surface beneath his body. Opening his eyes, he found himself lying on a black-and-white-checkered floor that stretched out beneath him like a giant chessboard. Breathing in the musty smell of leather and paper, he stood and turned full circle. A massive collection of books surrounded him.

Elaborately carved bookcases stretched up toward a stained-glass ceiling where the bright sunlight refracted through the panes of colored glass, illuminating the entire room. Each bookcase was filled with thousands of leather-bound books in horizontal rows. The volumes seemed identical at first, but when Harry moved closer, he realized that a different person's name was embossed on each of the leather bindings.

He walked through an archway into another enormous room and saw a long wooden help desk lining its east wall. Behind it sat a woman in a cream sweater sorting several piles of books. Her auburn hair was twisted up off her neck with a pencil.

The woman looked up as he approached.

"You must be Harry!" she said as she reached over the counter to shake his hand. "Let me be the first to welcome you back to the twenty-first century. I'm Cordelia, and I'll be your next trainer."

"What is this place?" Harry asked, unable to stop looking around.

"It's the Library of Influence," Cordelia replied. "Our mission is simple. We are committed to building a bulletproof case around the second principle of tribalry."

She put down the book in her hands and led Harry to the main hallway. Written along the wall behind her was the phrase "Every Opportunity Has Its Root in a Relationship."

"*Every* opportunity?" Harry echoed.

Cordelia looked amused. "That's exactly how I felt the first time I saw it—skeptical. I have an analytical mind, and that kind of absolute statement didn't sit well with me."

"Yeah, it doesn't sound right to me, either," Harry said. "Look at self-made people like Walt Disney and Thomas Edison."

"Do you really think either of those individuals succeeded by himself?" Cordelia asked.

"Well, you don't hear much about anyone else," Harry pointed out.

"You definitely came to the right place," Cordelia replied.

Harry wasn't ready to leave it at that.

"Okay, relationships probably played a role in their success," he persisted. "Maybe some of their best opportunities came from other people, but I'm sure there are plenty of opportunities that don't have anything to do with relationships. There certainly have been for me."

"Really?" A sparkle came into Cordelia's eyes, and Harry wondered if she were secretly laughing at him. "Like what?"

Harry took a second to think.

"Got one," he announced triumphantly. "My first job out of high school. I found it on an online job board."

"I can see how you would think that had nothing to do with relationships," Cordelia replied. She seemed to be choosing her words carefully. "But let me ask you a few questions. How did you discover the job site?"

As Harry thought about it, he remembered that his mother had heard about the website from one of her friends and had told Harry about it.

"My mom," Harry replied.

"Someone from your family tribe. Now, tell me about the job," Cordelia said.

"It was an auto repair shop," Harry replied.

"And you got that kind of job with no experience?" Cordelia asked, her eyebrows lifting in surprise.

"No," Harry admitted reluctantly. "My best friend Mark—his dad was an engineer. Our group of friends spent hours in his garage taking apart machinery and then putting it back together again. Mark's dad answered our questions when we couldn't figure things out."

"A club tribe," Cordelia observed. "Did you use your friend's father as a reference?"

Harry said he had.

"We've identified a couple of relationships that played a role in that opportunity, and I guarantee if we kept digging, we'd uncover many more," Cordelia said. "Walt Disney and other so-called 'self-made' individuals are no different. Follow me and I'll show you."

They passed a large number of bookcases as they walked over to the north wing, and Harry observed that each bookcase had a plaque identifying which individual it belonged to. They passed collections for many famous individuals, including George Washington, Marie Curie, Clarence Thomas, Rosa Parks, Mother Teresa, Jesse Owens, Mahatma Gandhi, Pelé, Red Cloud, Ludwig van Beethoven, Henry Ford, Meg Whitman, and Neil Armstrong. The shelves continued in every direction as far as Harry could see.

When he asked Cordelia about the books, she explained that the foundation had given her a grant to compile the world's largest collection of relationship histories.

"Every volume inside these collections represents a relationship the collection holder has," Cordelia told him. "Having strong relationships is much like having a living library. When you have a need, you have free access to the resources of your trusted tribe members to help you. It follows that the more books you have in your collection, the better your chances for success."

Harry tried to wrap his mind around what Cordelia was saying but was struggling to grasp everything.

"One way to better understand this principle is to play a game," Cordelia said. "It's a type of relationship scavenger hunt. Go and look through the collections and then bring me back some books you find interesting."

Harry looked down the long halls in dismay. "Where should I start?"

"You mentioned Walt Disney. His collection is right over there," she said, pointing to a massive wall full of books across the walkway.

Harry nodded, and as he got closer to the wooden bookshelves, he saw a plaque bearing the words: "The Walt Disney Collection." The books stretched up several stories and, curious about what names he'd find at the top, Harry pushed the wooden ladder along its track and climbed up to select a volume.

After exploring a variety of different collections, Harry finally returned with a stack of books. Sitting in the armchair across from Cordelia, he pushed them across the low table between them.

"What do we have here?" Cordelia asked, leaning forward to examine the spines of Harry's selections. She picked a book close to the top and said, "Let's start with this one. Ub Iwerks, from the Walt Disney collection."

"That's one unusual name," Harry commented.

Cordelia agreed as she opened the book. She showed Harry the sketches of different cartoon characters that filled the inside cover.

"Walt Disney wasn't a top-notch animator, and he knew it," Cordelia explained. "So, using all his powers of persuasion, Walt set out to convince friend and former partner Ub Iwerks to leave a high-paying job and relocate halfway across the country. Eventually he was successful and Ub became the studio's first chief animator."

Cordelia explained that the studio experienced some early success with a cartoon character named Oswald the Rabbit, but then disaster struck.   While Walt was in New York renegotiating their contract, his distributor informed Walt that not only was he taking Oswald away from him, but he'd also successfully recruited Walt's entire team of animators to join his staff.

"All of the animators except one, that is. Ub knew that staying with Walt meant he was now a staff of one, but he refused to desert his friend. On the train ride back from New York to California, Walt had an idea for a new character, and Ub drew him into life." Cordelia looked up at Harry mischievously. "Any guesses who that turned out to be?"

"No way. Mickey Mouse?" Harry asked.

Cordelia nodded. "Do you see where the principle 'Every opportunity has its root in a relationship' starts getting its teeth? Without Ub, there might have never been a Mickey Mouse."

Closing the book and placing it back on the table, Cordelia observed, "Ub Iwerks is a pretty important volume inside Walt's collection, wouldn't you say? And Ub is only one of thousands who lived inside of Walt Disney's work tribe."

Cordelia transitioned to the next volume, this time explaining how Estée Lauder's family tribe had launched her career. Estée's uncle, John Schotz, had taught his niece the secrets of skin care at a very young age, and together they'd concocted a snowy cream that made the skin feel like silk. It was that cream that became the foundation of the billion-dollar Estée Lauder empire.

Cordelia flipped through the pages of the next volume, entitled "Charles Taylor." Harry had picked it up from the joint shelves of the Orville and Wilbur Wright collection. Cordelia explained that when the Wright Brothers had discovered the engine they needed for their first flyer wasn't available in the United States, they enlisted the help of a member of their work tribe. Although Charley had originally been hired to fix bicycles inside their Dayton, Ohio, shop, the two brothers soon discovered he was a man of remarkable gifts. Working off rough sketches provided by the Wrights, Charley began crafting an engine prototype he finished in six weeks. He was the Wright's leading mechanic for years afterward, building engines for their daring exhibitions.

"Without Charley, it is possible that the Wright brothers might have been only a footnote in aviation history," Cordelia finished.

Harry exclaimed, "I can't believe I've never heard of these people before."

Picking up a volume from the Google section bearing the name David Cheriton, Cordelia explained, "When Larry Page and Sergey Brin needed funding to turn their doctoral project into an actual company, they turned to their Stanford tribe for help. Their faculty advisor, David Cheriton, agreed to introduce the two Google founders to his close friend, legendary Silicon Valley investor Andy Bechtolsheim. They arranged to meet early one morning on David's front porch. Huddled around a laptop, Andy got his first glimpse of Google's revolutionary search engine. When they finished, Andy said, 'I'm sure it will help you guys if I just write a check.' He went to retrieve his checkbook, and Larry and Sergey began to frantically discuss how much they should ask for. When Andy returned, he insisted they would need at least twice the amount they'd asked for and proceeded to write them a check for $100,000."

"The Thomas Edison collection," Cordelia murmured as she picked up another book from Harry's stack. "Edison is the epitome of the 'lone genius' in many people's minds, yet one of the inventions he's most celebrated for could've easily belonged to his rival, Alexander Graham Bell—if it hadn't been for Edison's work tribe."

Cordelia explained that after eleven years of perfecting his phonograph, Edison received the news that Bell was preparing to launch a phonograph that would best his own. He immediately called in his team for a "lock-in." Dozens of his employees, along with Edison himself, closed the doors of their West Orange lab—committed not to emerge until they had perfected the phonograph. Three sleepless days later, Edison and his bleary-eyed work tribe burst from the laboratory with a history-shaping, reinvented phonograph.

"Wow," Harry said under his breath, slowly shaking his head. He'd always viewed founders of major corporations and great innovators as coming from a different breed, assuming their successes were exclusively the result of their own relentless efforts and far-reaching vision. The realization that they'd created their empires by building effective tribes made them seem a little more human.

"Tommie Wilck, from the Disney tribe. I love a full-circle ending," Cordelia said, picking up the last volume.

After years of effort, Walt Disney had finally acquired the screen rights for the book Mary Poppins and needed to find an actress to play the lead role. They brainstormed and discarded different ideas until Walt's secretary, Tommie Wilck, suggested a young actress she'd recently seen on Broadway named Julie Andrews.

"And the rest is history. Mary Poppins made $44 million in its first release. It also garnered thirteen Academy Award nominations, one of which went to Hollywood newcomer Julie Andrews for best actress."

Cordelia closed the book and looked at Harry. "Our culture constantly celebrates the achievements of individuals, but no one has ever built something meaningful without the help of others. The truth is, we all need other people to play a role in our story."

"Okay, okay, I give up," Harry said, raising his hands in defeat. "Self-made success is a myth, just like Santa Claus."

"It might be better if we save that discussion for another time," Cordelia said, flashing him a bright smile.

As Harry helped Cordelia carry the books back to the sorting counter, Harry realized how seldom he'd considered the contributions of other people in his life.

As if reading his thoughts, Cordelia asked, "Would you like to see your own collection?"

Harry looked around eagerly. "Mine? You have a section for me?"

"My newest one," Cordelia said over her shoulder. She motioned for Harry to follow her down the corridor. They trekked to the other side of the sprawling north wing and finally stopped in front of a wall modestly stocked with several hundred books.

"Not exactly Walt Disney, but here it is. The Harry Green Collection," Cordelia announced with a flourish. "You will find individual volumes for your family members, friends, teachers, classmates, coworkers, clients, vendors, teammates, and neighbors. Each significant relationship is represented."

As Harry scanned through the names, Cordelia said, "Harry, let's play the game one more time. Find a name you don't know."

Harry looked confused. "But this is my collection. Shouldn't I know all of the names?"

"Just try it," she insisted.

Harry got up and slowly skimmed through the book titles, then he reached down and pulled a book from the bottom shelf.

"Ted Jacobson? Who's he?" Harry asked, looking down at the book in confusion.

"Ted Jacobson," Cordelia said, wrinkling her forehead reflectively. She took the book from Harry and started flipping through the pages. "He's the director of the Oak Grove Intramural Softball League."

"Oh, that Ted. We played on a team together one year." Harry stopped to think. "I don't think I ever knew his last name."

"Some people think he's a little unusual, don't they?" Cordelia asked, holding open a page that had a full-length photo of Ted. He was tall and lanky, and his sandy blond hair fell into his eyes.

"Yeah, I guess," Harry agreed. "A lot of people don't give him the time of day, but he's actually a really great guy."

Harry searched his memory for opportunities that came from Ted but drew a blank.

Cordelia finally asked him if he remembered Ted asking him to fill an empty spot on a corporate team the Oak Grove Community Bank had put together. Harry nodded; he'd scored a home run at one of the tournament games. Suddenly it clicked.

"The Lions!" Harry exclaimed, throwing up his hands in triumph. "That's where I met Vince."

Cordelia pointed out that Vince was not only one of Harry's good friends but also one of his most important business associates.

She pulled Vince's book off the shelf and added, "Vince was instrumental in getting the loans you needed to later finance Dillon-Parker, and he also introduced you to another key business relationship."

Harry instantly realized who Cordelia was referring to.

"Jackson. I met Jackson while we were serving on the board of Vince's nonprofit." Harry was shocked he'd never made the connection before.

"You have Jackson, partner and half owner of your business, because of Vince. And you know Vince because Ted Jacobson invited you to join a sport tribe," Cordelia pointed out.

"I should probably send him a thank-you note or something," Harry said, trying to remember the last time he'd talked to Ted.

"Remember how Afu explained to you that tribes are often built on reciprocal exchanges? They often happen without us even realizing it," Cordelia commented as she retrieved three more volumes from a nearby table and presented them to Harry. Etched onto their leather spines were Patrick's, Afu's, and Cordelia's names.

"Go ahead and put them on the shelf, Harry. The three of us are now members of your foundation tribe."

Cordelia asked Harry to follow her up a nearby flight of stairs, picking up a volume from the Queen Victoria collection on the way. They stopped at a small balcony overlooking the library.

As they stood side by side, looking out over the collections, Cordelia said, "Harry, the purpose of this library is to help you understand a principle that isn't usually talked about in school. The principle is this: Individual resources are never enough. Success in life swings on the hinge of a thousand key relationships."

Cordelia opened up the book she'd picked up and passed it to Harry. "Henry Melvill was a chaplain for Queen Victoria and one of the greatest rhetoricians of his time. I think he sums up this principle nicely."

She pointed at some highlighted text, and Harry read the marked passage aloud. "We cannot live for ourselves alone. Our lives are connected by a thousand invisible threads."

Harry sat staring at the words for a moment. A bell signaled the passing of the hour, and Cordelia smiled up at Harry. "Well, now, George Bailey, it looks like you've realized what a wealthy man you are."

"Yeah, it's a wonderful life, Clarence," Harry replied with a wry grin.

7.
Avoid Relationship Arrogance

The raggy colt often makes a handsome horse.

—Irish Proverb

Seconds later, Harry found himself back in his den. Glad to be home, he sank back into the soft leather of his chair, feeling inspired, confused, and frustrated all at the same time.

Reviewing his business career, Harry recalled the many times he'd acted like a gladiator and the occasional times he'd been more like a tribe leader. *What if this really is the answer?* Harry asked himself, feeling one of his pounding headaches coming on.

Part of him didn't want it to be the answer. Building a tribe took time, and time was something he didn't have. As he thought this, he felt a sharp spasm of pain shoot through his heart.

"Ow!" Harry cried, pressing down on his chest to ease the throbbing. His vision began to blur, and everything went dark.

He felt a heavy pressure on his tongue and saw a sudden burst of light.

"Say ahhh," a voice directed.

"Whaaaaa—?" Harry replied, gagging on the tongue depressor.

The light switched off, and when the purple spots that were left by the bright lights cleared, Harry discovered he was sitting on the white paper of an examination table. The tongue depressor operator stood before him, dressed in green scrubs, her wiry black hair tied back from her face.

She scrawled a few notations on a clipboard and said, "Now then, Mr. Green—may I call you Harry?"

"Sure," Harry said, dragging his eyes away from a nearby canister of hypodermic syringes.

"My name is Dr. Angela Peterman, and I'm your next trainer," she said, shaking his hand. "It's a pleasure to meet you, though I do wish it was under more favorable circumstances."

This sounded ominous, and the thin paper crackled beneath Harry as he shifted nervously.

"I'm afraid I have some bad news for you," the doctor continued. "You're suffering from a severe case of RA."

Harry felt the blood drain out of his face, and he braced himself for the worst. "I knew something was wrong. Is it serious?"

"It definitely can be," the doctor affirmed.

"What is it?" Harry asked, struggling to keep his voice steady.

The doctor suggested that he take a seat on one of the more comfortable chairs that lined the perimeter of the examination room. She waited until he was settled before continuing.

"RA stands for relationship arrogance, and although common, it can be deadly," Angela said. "I could give you a highly technical explanation, but I think it'll make more sense if I use an example."

Angela directed Harry's attention to a dark-paneled x-ray box on the wall across from him that had a large negative clipped to it. When Angela turned on the backlight, it revealed a photograph of a group of people sitting around a table, eating lunch. Recognizing himself in the picture, Harry realized that it had been taken at the office's monthly birthday lunch. Harry hadn't attended for a while but had finally made time to come to this one.

Popping the top off a black marker, Angela handed it to Harry. "I want you to circle the two people you were focusing on at this lunch."

Harry circled two people in the photograph.

"Why did you choose them?" Angela asked.

"The first one is a director who is currently considering an offer from another company, and the other is my sales manager. I was trying to encourage him to hit his numbers this month," Harry responded.

Angela uncapped another marker—this one red—and crossed out the other three individuals sitting near him. She pointed to one crossed-out individual, a middle-aged man with a beard who sat next to Harry at the table.

"What about him?" she asked. "Why didn't you take the time to get to know him?"

Harry looked at the man's face, trying to remember who he was. "He's a new hire in our finance department," Harry finally said, shrugging his shoulders dismissively. "I don't even know if we're going to be able to keep him."

"Don't you like him?" Angela persisted. "His name is David Edwards, by the way."

"He seemed nice enough," Harry said, a note of defensiveness creeping into his voice. "He reminded me of my uncle Mac."

Angela made no comment but continued gazing steadily at Harry.

When the silence became uncomfortable, Harry explained, "I came to try to keep my star players from leaving. I wasn't going to waste my time talking to someone who may not even be around in a few months."

Tapping Harry's chest with the marker, Angela said, "So you're basically saying that he didn't have what you wanted. But are you aware of anything that *he* needed?"

Harry looked back at the picture of David Edwards, trying to remember their short conversation.

"Yeah, I guess he mentioned something," Harry admitted. "It crossed my mind to arrange to have some key people from sales and customer service brainstorm with him on a project he was struggling with."

Nodding, Angela asked, "So why didn't you offer to do that?"

"I was focusing on the others."

Angela apparently didn't realize how close to bankruptcy his business was.

"The definition of relationship arrogance is prioritizing relationships based on a forecasted return on investment," Angela said. She turned off the backlight, and the picture faded into the dark panel.

Angela pulled out a CAT scan of Harry's upper body and pointed to his chest area. "The infection started in your heart and has corrupted your vision. When you meet people, you prioritize their worth based on whether you think they can help you achieve your immediate objectives."

Harry opened his mouth to protest that this wasn't true, but as he tried to cite examples to argue his case, he found himself at a loss.

"But I can't talk *every* day with *every* person in the company," he finally responded. "That's just not possible."

"I'm not saying you can or should," Angela said. "I'm saying that the way you judge people affects your ability to build a relationship with them and that it's arrogant to make assumptions before having any meaningful interaction. Also, as the tribe leader, you set the tone and standard for how your staff will interact with each other when you model relationship arrogance."

Angela walked to the opposite end of the examination room and stood by a metal vault that hadn't been there before.

"On the other side of this door are the results of your tribe scan," she said, pulling out a card with a magnetic strip. "I've gotten clearance for us to go inside."

Angela slid the card through an electronic scanner, and the light on the handle flashed green as the thick door swung open on huge hinges. They stepped into a long hallway filled with different doorways. Above each doorframe were signs for the different tribes Harry belonged to: his family, his company, the softball league, the animal rescue board, his design association, his neighborhood, his church, his entrepreneurial group, his business school alumni, and all of his previous jobs.

"Since we're focusing on Dillon-Parker, let's choose that door."

Harry turned the knob, and it swung open to reveal a cavernous room. Harry saw a myriad of three-dimensional holographic images of his employees—each one actively engaged in some kind of activity. The images were talking on their phones, driving their cars, sitting in business meetings, and working at their desks. In columns behind them were holograms of hundreds of other people.

"What is this place?" Harry asked.

"It's a visual representation of the relationships inside the Dillon-Parker tribe. Every tribe member is represented, and the people inside their spheres of influence are lined up behind them."

Wandering through the room, Harry stopped in front of a woman who was waterskiing and called out, "Sandy, our receptionist, knows Anna Baird! She used to be my real estate agent. Wow, this place is like a funhouse on steroids."

"Harry," Angela called out from the other side of the room. "Come over here and see this."

Harry made his way through the maze of holograms, walking past a couple sitting hunched down in their seats in a movie theater, their wide eyes glued to the screen. He walked by a woman interviewing a nervous-looking young man for a job. As he continued, he recognized David Edwards working at his computer and ran into Angela about halfway down the column of people behind David. She stood next to the image of a man talking to a bank teller.

"Harry, allow me to introduce you to someone," Angela said with a flourish. "I don't think you've met Will Clay."

"Will Clay?" Harry repeated, shocked at seeing the business owner he'd been trying to connect with for six months.

Angela permitted herself a small smile. "Will Clay is David's neighbor. Their families go camping together every year."

Harry closed his eyes and groaned softly.

"Relationship arrogance tends to be the principle of tribalry that cuts straight to the heart," Angela said, patting Harry's shoulder sympathetically. She steered Harry out of the tribe scan and back into the stark examination room. "I think you'd better sit down," she suggested, a worried look on her face.

"I'm an idiot," Harry said, burying his face in his hands.

"Yes, you are. But I wouldn't feel too bad about it. So is almost everyone else. Self-interest is the sole motivation of gladiators, and if they can't forecast a quick return on a relationship, they discard the relationship and move on. But what they don't understand is that every person has hidden influence we can't see."

Harry replayed the lunch in his mind, wondering how he would've done things differently if only he could've seen David's connection with Will Clay.

"At this point, I should warn you of another pitfall. When you begin to understand that everyone has hidden influence, there's a temptation to build a relationship simply to access it. Building relationships with this motivation is also problematic—because you're still forecasting a return on your investment. People can sense that kind of thing and will instinctively distrust you."

Angela picked up a pad of paper and scribbled on it. "I'm going to refer you to one of our specialists—our very best, in fact. He can treat even the most serious cases of relationship arrogance."

She ripped off the slip of paper with practiced efficiency and handed a prescription to Harry. As she did this, Harry heard the printer in the corner come on; it spit out a piece of paper.

"Oh, I almost forgot. You also need your receipt," she said, picking up the paper and handing it to him.

Looking at the total, Harry started to panic. "This is over $800,000. I can't pay this!"

"Don't worry. It's a receipt, not a bill. And you've already paid it in full," Angela reassured him. "That's the amount relationship arrogance has already cost your business in lost opportunities. Unfortunately, we have no way of calculating the personal costs, but I can assure you those are even more severe."

8.
Just Because

What is in the marrow is hard to take out of the bone.

—Irish Proverb

As he stared blankly at the total on the receipt, Harry sensed he'd changed locations once again. Looking up, he found himself standing beside Patrick at the center of a shopping mall. They were waiting near the front of a long line of eager children and their parents. The line wound through a white picket fence enclosing nine mechanical reindeer and two giant candy canes.

Harry looked around incredulously. "What happened to October and November? I swear it was September this morning."

Patrick shook his head. "You've already traveled back hundreds of years tonight. Don't tell me going forward a few months is going to put you in a state."

As he said this, the line moved, and Patrick nudged Harry forward.

"Wait a second. What are we doing?" Harry asked, stepping back and looking at Patrick suspiciously.

"We're goin' to a specialist to learn the next principle of tribalry," Patrick said, pointing to the raised platform where Santa Claus sat inside his sleigh, his snowy beard spilling out over his red velvet suit. "You're sure to like him. The man's a saint."

Harry felt like he'd jumped into a Christmas TV special, complete with all the clichéd trimmings. He slapped a hand against his forehead and started to laugh.

"You're putting me on, right? Now Santa's going to help me save my business? And look, Rudolph and Frosty are here too," Harry said in mock celebration, pointing to the fiberglass figurines in the Christmas display.

A marching band suddenly struck up "Deck the Halls," and people dressed as gingerbread cookies began throwing out gifts to the crowd. The line instantly broke up, leaving Harry standing alone at the front.

"Santa," Patrick said, pushing Harry forward a little, "I'm not sure this lad remembers knowing you, so it'll be my pleasure to reintroduce you. Harry, I'd like you to meet Kris Kringle."

Still shaking his head in disbelief, Harry looked up into a pair of brilliant blue eyes. Their gaze locked, and Harry felt a flood of childlike happiness sweep through him.

"Well, well, if it isn't Harry Green. It's a pleasure to see you again," said Kris, his deep voice ringing as he spoke.

A memory flitted at the edges of Harry's consciousness, but when he tried to pin it down, it slipped away.

Kris stroked his beard and began to chuckle. "I'm afraid you're going to have to climb up here to talk with me. Don't worry, you can sit there," he said pointing to the vacant space across from him on the sleigh. "You're getting a little big for my knee."

Harry felt embarrassment surge through his rapidly reddening cheeks, but in his mind's eye, he saw his signature at the bottom of the training contract, so he pulled himself up into the sleigh.

Kris's voice softened with sympathy. "This has been an especially rough year for you, hasn't it?"

Harry nodded, his eyes downcast.

"So, what can I do for you? I'm at your service," Kris said, his hands indicating his readiness.

"Anything?" Harry said, looking up at Kris in surprise.

"I'll do my best," Kris promised.

Harry looked over at Patrick doubtfully, and Patrick nodded encouragingly. "Go ahead, lad. You know what you've been wanting."

"I want to get the Clay & Chagall account. I think it might help save my business," Harry told him.

Kris let out a low whistle and leaned back against the shellacked backboard of the sleigh. "That's a pretty tall order. Tell me more about it."

As Harry described Dillon-Parker's struggles, he got the distinct impression that Kris had cleared his mind and was devoting his full attention to what Harry was telling him. When he finished, Kris asked Harry for the prescription Dr. Angela had given him.

Kris skimmed through it, then turned to Patrick. "My friend, it's time for my supper, and I'm tired of the Corn Dog Palace. I've actually been craving some of your wife's Irish stew."

"Molly'll be delighted to have you both!" Patrick exclaimed. "And she'll feed you a feast that'll hold you through the longest day."

The next thing Harry knew, he was looking up at a cluster of copper kettles hanging from the iron ceiling rods of an elaborate kitchen. On the counter in front of him sat large piles of round potatoes, leafy lettuce, and fat, orange carrots.

Kris cleared his throat, and Harry followed his gaze to where a petite woman was standing on a squat, three-legged stool, reaching for something on the top shelf of a cupboard. Alerted to their arrival, Molly turned and stared at the three of them, dumbfounded. Then, letting out a wail, she lit into her husband.

"Glory be, Patrick! You need to be warning me when you're bringing home guests. I'm a sight to be seen!"

Brushing back an auburn curl from her glistening forehead, Molly tried unsuccessfully to smooth it back into her bun.

"It's my fault," Kris broke in, stepping forward to take the blame. "I was craving some of your divine stew. I hope I'm not putting you out."

Molly instantly softened. She gave the old man a hug, then stood back and looked him over. "Sure, and your looking like you haven't eaten in ages. I'll be warming up some supper directly."

Turning to Harry, she took both of his hands in her tiny ones, her eyes bright with tears. "And Harry! My, but you do have the look of your great-great-grandfather to you," she commented, her eyes never leaving his face. "It's glad I am to finally meet you. Patrick's been telling me what a quick learner you're turning out to be now that the famous Green stubbornness is wearing off."

Harry laughed. "Thank you . . . I think."

Patrick took charge of setting the table, and as Harry helped him put out the knives and forks, he stole a quick peek out the kitchen window. He saw a shady lane filled with beautiful homes, but before he could inquire about their exact location, he was distracted by a mouth-watering smell. Molly had lifted the lid off the large pot sitting on the stove, and as its succulent blend of bacon, garlic, and spices wafted through the kitchen, Harry's stomach let out a growl.

"I see you've inherited the Green appetite as well," Molly observed with a laugh. She dipped her wooden spoon into the stew and tasted it critically. "Not me finest, but it'll have to do. Let's get some nourishment into you."

The group gathered around the cozy kitchen table to eat. The dinner conversation centered on Harry's training thus far, as Molly passed out generous helpings of stew and thick slices of brown soda bread.

When they finished eating, Patrick and Molly began to clear the table, insisting that they would clean up and that Harry and Kris should use the time to talk.

"Courtesy is no more important than wisdom," Patrick said firmly, pushing Harry back in his seat as he attempted to clear his plate. "Kris has things to tell you, things to say."

As the two men sat among the remains of the feast, Kris sighed contentedly and let out his belt a couple of notches. He then drew out Angela's prescription and read over it again.

"Did Angela explain that the occurrence of relationship arrogance is especially high among gladiators?" he asked.

"No, but that would make sense," Harry replied, remembering how every thought in his head had been riveted on his own survival when he'd been battling in the coliseum.

"People can usually spot a gladiator a mile away. They view others as human ATMs whose sole purpose is dispensing money and opportunities to them." Kris paused for a long moment, then finally said, "That brings me to a difficult issue. Tell me, Harry, why do you want to get to know Will Clay?"

It was as though Kris had punched him in the stomach. The blood drained from Harry's face, and he was unable to meet Kris's eyes. He finally whispered, "Because I think he can help me get me what I want."

He felt a hand on his shoulder, and Harry looked up to see that Kris's face was filled with understanding. "Relationship arrogance is as common as the cold, Harry. But that doesn't stop it from having devastating consequences. When people are constantly forecasting their return on investment, they become blind to the person behind the transaction, and this blindness renders them incapable of building real relationships."

Harry sat silently struggling with the emotions welling up inside him.

Finally Kris spoke. "Tell me this, Harry. Why am I helping you?"

Before Harry could answer, a billowing gray mist engulfed them. Eventually, the outlines of an adult and several small children appeared and gradually came into focus. Harry realized he was seeing himself lying on his living room floor, wrestling with his pint-sized daughters. He tickled them as they screamed with laughter.

"This was last Sunday," Harry told Kris. "I was supposed to be getting them ready for bed."

After the giggling stopped, Harry watched himself gather his youngest daughter in his arms.

"Sophie, why do I love you? Is it because of your big blue eyes?" he asked.

"No, Daddy!" the little girl exclaimed. She obviously knew this game.

"No?" Harry said, scratching his head in confusion. "Then I must love you because of how smart you are."

The little girl began to wriggle in delight, shouting out, "No!"

"Oh, now I remember," Harry said. "It's because you are such a good daughter."

"No, that's not why!" she said, falling to the floor in a heap of giggles.

Harry picked her up and set her back on her feet again. "Then why do I love you?" he asked.

"You love me just because I'm me!"

"Right! And what about you, Lynn?" Harry said, pulling another daughter to his side.

"You love me just because I'm me, too, Dad," she said, rolling her eyes but smiling.

"Me too! You love me just because, too!" May and Lauren chimed in.

Laughing, the girls tackled Harry and piled on top of him.

His wife walked in and began scolding them but was obviously having difficulty maintaining her stern expression. "It is an hour past your bedtime, girls. Kiss your dad good night and get in bed."

As the girls scampered up the stairs, Harry found himself sitting with Kris on a bench back at the mall.

"Harry, why am I helping you?" Kris asked again.

Harry suddenly had a hard time swallowing. "Just because I'm me?"

"Yes. Just because you're you. Building relationships 'just because' is the antidote for relationship arrogance. It feels pretty different when someone is getting to know you 'just because,' doesn't it?"

Harry nodded.

"Tribe leaders don't force residents to belong to their tribes. People choose to be a part of a tribe because it is led by someone who genuinely cares about them," Kris explained. "Everyone deserves to be treated that way, including Will Clay."

Harry paused for a moment before finally voicing a question that had been bothering him.

"Are you saying I should never develop a relationship with someone I think can help me?"

Kris threw back his head and laughed until his stomach jiggled.

"Of course not. I'm here to help save your business, not to grab a shovel and throw dirt on the coffin. Tribe leaders understand that they will benefit from building strong relationships; the difference is that they don't build those relationships with specific outcomes in mind. While they know that opportunities will flow as a result of the newly acquired trust, they haven't predetermined what those will look like. They build relationships just because they value people, plain and simple."

"I'm still not quite sure I understand. I mean, I get that Santa Claus does things just because, and I care about my children just because, but translating that into other relationships . . . ?"

"Can you think of a time where you've built a relationship without a forecasted return on investment?" Kris said. "For example, let's go back to Ted Jacobson with the Oak Grove Softball League. Why did you build a relationship with him?"

Harry thought about Ted. "He's just a good guy. I really like him."

"You realized tonight that he was instrumental in helping you with your business, but how did you help him first?"

"I don't remember . . ." Harry began but stopped when he realized what Kris was referring to.

Ted and Harry had got to talking after a game, and Ted mentioned he'd always wanted to put together a corporate softball league, but didn't know where to begin. Harry suggested having a corporate sports challenge to give companies the experience of playing together without having to make a commitment. Harry's company was the first to sign up, and he spread the word about the challenge to all his clients and vendors with his personal endorsement. More than half the teams that signed up were Harry's contacts.

"So, you helped Ted 'just because,' and that action came back to serve you in a way you never could've imagined," Kris said.

Harry thought about the opportunity Ted gave him to play on the newly formed Oak Grove Bank Team, and the resulting relationships with Vince and Jackson, and he had to agree.

"Ted knew you were looking to eventually strike out on your own and when he saw an opportunity to help you by giving you a chance to build relationships with the top bank in the area, he acted. Why? Because he trusted and liked you."

"It almost sounds too simple," Harry said.

Kris grasped Harry by the shoulders with his big hands and gave him a penetrating look. "Simple. Not easy. Would it have been easy for you to put the needs of David Edwards ahead of your own the other day?"

Harry sighed. "No."

Kris's smile poured over Harry like a warm shower. "It's more of a process than an event. It's taken me almost four centuries to perfect, but even though building relationships 'just because' will require effort, I know you can do it. I believe in you."

Harry silently watched as Kris walked back to the sleigh and lifted the first little girl in line onto his lap.

"You look like a ballerina to me," Harry heard him say.

A pleased smile broke over the little girl's face as she nodded.

"Didn't I say you'd like him?" Patrick said, appearing at Harry's side.

"How can you resist someone who likes you 'just because'?" Harry sighed, holding up his hands in defeat.

9.
Learn, Serve, Grow

When the apple is ripe, it will fall.

—Irish Proverb

"You're looking a bit haggard, lad," Patrick said, a note of concern in his voice. "We've a few minutes to spare. Why don't you take a break."

Harry nodded gratefully. Patrick showed him to the bathroom. Flipping on the light, Harry examined himself in the mirror.

"You look like you've been hit by a truck," he told his reflection.

His hair was matted down, sticking out in odd places, and dark circles had formed underneath his eyes. Harry knew these signs of exhaustion weren't only the result of tonight's adventures; he'd been burning the candle at both ends for almost a year now, and it was starting to show.

He turned the silver handle of the faucet and held a washcloth under the stream of cold water. As he rubbed the cloth over his face, he heard the muffled clanging of the clock in Patrick's front hall.

When he lowered the cloth, Harry looked in the mirror and let out a startled yelp, stumbling backward. As he fell he tipped over the large garbage can that had appeared behind him. Wadded-up paper towels and pieces of chewing gum spilled out across the tile floor of a public bathroom.

Harry straightened himself and scrambled back to the mirror. Running his fingers over his face in awe, he stared at a teenage version of himself. Not only had the dark circles disappeared, but the fine lines that had formed over the last fifteen years had vanished as well.

Behind him, a short young man with carrot-red hair entered the bathroom and approached the sink next to Harry.

"Top of the morning to you, lad," he said as he filled his hands with soap from the dispenser. "You're the spitting image of your great-uncle Calvin at this age."

"Patrick? Is that you?" Harry's gaze jerked away from his own reflection to stare at the boy beside him. "You look like you're twelve."

Patrick lifted up his chin, clearly offended. "I'm nearly sixteen, and I took enough bashing 'bout my size from the lads down in the village, so there's no need for you to be adding your two bits."

Patrick dried his hands and motioned for Harry to follow him.

"Where are we going?" Harry asked nervously, suddenly seized with the fear that he might have to relive his formative years.

"'Tis a fine day for a ramble down memory lane," Patrick said, holding open the bathroom door for Harry.

Seeing no alternative, Harry followed Patrick out into a large hallway lined with lockers and classrooms.

"Oak Grove High," Harry muttered, looking around in awe. "I'm back in high school."

As he walked down the hall, Harry began experiencing some benefits from this plunge back into his youth. His energy seemed to increase with every step, and his adult troubles melted away. Even his perpetual tension headache had disappeared.

The bell rang, releasing rush hour. Every inch of the hallway was suddenly filled with teenagers. Harry began pointing out his old classmates to Patrick as they walked down the hall.

"Do you see that girl across the hall, over in the corner?" Harry asked.

Patrick looked over to where a vivacious brunette with a mouthful of braces stood surrounded by a group of friends.

"You mean the one talkin' and talkin'?" Patrick finally asked after observing her tell a detailed story without taking a breath. "Does she ever come up for air?"

"Nope, it's my little sister Amy, and oxygen only slows her down."

As if by instinct, Harry stopped at his old locker and began twisting the dial to see if he could remember his combination.

"Green Machine!" a voice from behind him called out.

Instantly responding to his nickname, Harry turned around to see Mark Child, his best friend since high school, standing before him. Automatically, he put his hand out to perform their signature handshake.

"Mark! It's so good to see you!" Harry exclaimed.

Shooting him a look that plainly asked whether he'd lost his mind, Mark responded, "Yeah . . . it's good to see you too. That whole class period away from you was rough."

Then his face suddenly cracked into a grin, and he threw an arm around Harry's shoulder, playfully jabbing him in the ribs. "I'm just giving you a hard time, man. Hopefully next time I won't have to go to these kinds of extremes to spend some time with you."

Harry stopped dead and looked over at Mark. "Wait a second," he said. "Are you telling me that *you're* my next trainer?"

"A rookie, true, but fully certified; I completed the training a couple of years ago," Mark told him. "When the foundation asked me where I wanted to hold my session of your training, I couldn't think of a better place then good ol' Oak Grove High."

Looking back and forth between Mark and Patrick, a suspicion suddenly sprouted inside Harry's brain. "You didn't have anything to do with me being—er . . . selected for this training, did you Mark?"

"What are friends for?" he replied with a wicked grin. "C'mon, let's get going."

"Where are we going?" Harry asked.

"Well, technically you're supposed to be in English reciting 'The Road Less Traveled,' but somehow I don't think you're up to that today, so let's go to first lunch instead."

"I'll be leavin' you to it," Patrick said, disappearing into the crowd of students.

Mark and Harry walked into the huge commons area at the center of the school, and they saw teenagers of all shapes and sizes lounging on the carpeted risers or standing in tight clusters along the walls. The area was divided into the well-defined territories of the athletes, the brains, the rebels, and the drama and music crowds.

"Look at all of us," Harry said, taking a seat on a riser that had a panoramic view of the entire room. "It's like we thought we'd come down with an infectious disease if we talked to someone we didn't know."

"We were all pretty insecure that's for sure," Mark agreed as he lounged back on his elbows beside Harry. "So, how have things been going so far?" he asked curiously.

"Pretty good, actually. I'm starting to understand why it's important to build relationships and what my objectives should be," Harry said. "But I'm still a little hazy on how I'm supposed to consciously go out and do it. Don't relationships just happen?"

"Sure," Mark replied, "but understanding how relationships naturally develop can show you how to build them intentionally. This is essential because the primary responsibility of a tribe leader is to help tribe members build relationships with each other. Tribe members do this by practicing the last principle of tribalry: learn, serve, grow."

Mark stopped and seemed to make up his mind about something.

"At this point, I could just talk you through the process of building a relationship, but I think it'll make more sense if you experience it firsthand."

Behind them, there was a sudden commotion, and Harry turned to see four large boys herding a smaller boy around the corner.

"Hey, that looks like . . ." Harry turned back to Mark, his eyebrows shooting up. "You chose that day, huh?"

Mark nodded affirmatively.

"I'll be back," Harry told him.

Harry sprinted down the hallway and around a corner. As he rounded the bend, he saw a pair of legs sticking out of a garbage can. He broke through the pack that surrounded the garbage can and placed himself between it and the boys.

"Do you guys know why my friends call me the Green Machine?" he asked, nose to nose with the largest boy.

"No. Why don't you tell us," the boy replied jeeringly, trying unsuccessfully to match Harry's intensity.

"It's because I can rip a bully like you apart in about thirty seconds. Believe me, I'm not somebody you want to mess with."

The boy breathed heavily through his nose, sizing Harry up. Then he broke eye contact and turned back to his friends. "C'mon, let's go. This guy's a freak."

Harry turned to find that the boy had extricated himself from the garbage can and was cleaning off his thick glasses with the edge of his shirt.

"You all right?" Harry asked

"Yeah, I guess," the boy muttered, but when he saw Harry's expression, he added, "Don't worry, this is a pretty normal first day. I should be used to it by now."

He looked down and kicked the floor in frustration.

"Let's get out of here," Harry said, jerking his chin in the direction of the commons.

As they walked down the hallway, the boy asked, "So, what's your real name?"

"What? Oh . . . I'm Harry. Harry Green."

"I'm Darrin Clark," the boy said. "I just transferred here from Texas, but I'm not from there either. I'm not from anywhere, really. My dad is in the military, so we move around a lot."

As they neared the commons, Darrin's body became more and more translucent until he eventually disappeared altogether. Harry looked around and saw Mark waving him over.

"I haven't talked to Darrin in years. Have you heard from him lately?" Harry asked as he sat down.

"I talked to him last week," Mark said. "He and his wife just moved, and I called to get their new address. As we were talking about old times, your Superman heroics came up. I realized I'd never asked you why you did it."

"Back before you knew me, I was a pretty chubby kid and dealt with more than my fair share of bullies," Harry explained, staring down the group of offending boys as they slunk back into the commons area. "Ever since, I've had zero tolerance for the creeps."

"The same process that helped you develop a friendship with Darrin is the same process you'd use to build one with anyone else, so let's analyze it. How did Darrin transition from being the kid in the garbage can to being part of our friend tribe?"

Unzipping his backpack, Mark took out a marker and then grabbed a banner from a pile of discarded dance decorations. He wrote "Learn" on the back of it.

"Learning is the beginning stage of all relationships—learning what people like, don't like, or how they think and feel. It's especially important during this stage to try and understand the other person's wants and needs," Mark explained. "So what kinds of things did you learn about Darrin that first day?"

Harry immediately thought about what Darrin had said to him in the hallway.

"I learned that his dad was in the military and he'd never stayed at the same school for more than a couple of years. Because of that, making friends didn't come easily to him. Oh, and of course it only took a few hours of hanging out with him to discover his addiction to soda," Harry said, ticking off the different pieces of information on his fingers as he listed them.

Recalling the first time he'd seen his new friend's bedroom, Harry remembered the national awards from chess tournaments that covered every inch of wall space, giving Harry his first clue that his new friend was a master strategist.

"Good," Mark said when Harry mentioned this, "but you're still missing something. As our friend tribe got to know Darrin better, we heard more than we ever wanted to hear about something that was *really* important to him."

Mark pointed to where a petite blonde sat eating her lunch with the tennis team.

"Melanie Harris," Harry said and slowly began to grin. "How could I forget? He was the brain, and she was the athlete, and the whole thing being completely hopeless just seemed to make him like her more."

"As you learn about people, you'll eventually discover specific wants or needs they have, like you did with Darrin. This is critical because identifying what someone needs, then helping them get it, will build a relationship faster than anything else."

Mark uncapped the lid of another marker and wrote "Serve" in big letters below "Learn."

"So, how did you help Darrin with Melanie?"

"Wait a second, that was a group effort," Harry protested. "I may have brought the issue to everyone's attention, but if I remember, inviting her to an all-night Risk tournament and putting her on Darrin's team was your idea."

"I'll never forget them crushing the rest of us into a bloody pulp as they ruthlessly conquered the world," Mark reminisced.

"End result: they dated all senior year. Mission accomplished," Harry said, wiping his hands in satisfaction over a job well done.

Mark added that although helping other people to achieve specific wants and needs was often the fastest way to build a relationship, there were other ways to serve as well. Being genuinely interested in what people had to say, spending time with them, or remembering important events—all were "serves" because each of these actions built higher levels of trust.

Mark then wrote "Grow" underneath the words "Learn" and "Serve."

"Can you think of opportunities that came to you because of your friendship with Darrin?" Mark asked.

"Yeah, when I ran for student-body president," Harry said instantly. "The rest of you were good for a few laughs, but it was Darrin who got me elected."

Harry remembered how Darrin had transformed his bedroom into campaign headquarters. It had looked like he was planning a full military coup with all the graphs, charts, and slogans.

"I know his dad was pretty high up in the military," Harry recalled. "But I still don't know how he was able to swing getting a tank. I'll never forget the day he parked it on the high school patio, completely covered with banners that said 'Vote for the Green Machine.'"

"The other candidates didn't stand a chance," Mark said, shaking his head.

"Nope, it was shock and awe from beginning to end," Harry agreed, grinning as he remembered the crowds of kids swarming around the tank at lunch hour. "Darrin also spent hours coaching me on my speech. It was his idea to give it like a drill sergeant."

Harry could still see himself on the stage, bellowing out orders to the student body. It had been one of the most memorable moments of his life, and he had Darrin to thank for it.

"That speech is an Oak Grove High legend," Mark agreed.

"But we were friends," Harry said, suddenly realizing what Mark was getting at. "I didn't build a relationship with him so I could win an election, and I would've still been his friend even if he hadn't helped me." "Relax. We're dissecting a natural phenomenon here," Mark explained. "When you effectively learn about people and serve them 'just because,' they naturally want to reciprocate and help you accomplish your goals as well. That's just how the 'grow' part of the cycle works."

Harry hadn't really thought of it that way. *The end result of learning and serving was that people just wanted to help you, even if that wasn't your intent in building the relationship in the first place?*

"The learn, serve, grow cycle describes the process of building sustainable relationships. As you and your tribe members continue to learn and serve 'just because,' you'll gain greater access to the time, influence, and resources of each other. But remember, it's a cycle, and just like any other cycle, it needs to be repeated over and over again to keep the relationship strong."

Learn, serve, grow. It seemed fairly straightforward to Harry.

Mark looked out over the sea of faces in the commons and pointed out a pretty, dark-haired girl who was flirting with one of the basketball players.

"If I remember, Stacy Reynolds was your favorite subject in high school. I'll never forget the day you finally got up the courage to ask her to the Homecoming dance."

A flood of memories washed over Harry. Stacy Reynolds! She hadn't crossed his mind in years, yet in high school she'd been all he could think about. Midterms, gym class, and homework he could do without, but he suddenly missed the rush of wondering if she would ever give him the time of day.

"Yeah, I waited my entire high school career to go out with her, and when she was finally my girlfriend, everything fell apart." Harry still remembered his frustration at the situation. "She made me cookies, left me notes, and would call me, but whenever I tried to do things for her, I could see her get worried, like I was going to think she was a burden or something. It got so one-sided I finally had to end it."

"She didn't understand the law of grow," Mark said. "Relationships are strongest when balanced. Making continual demands on a relationship will weaken it, but so will never allowing the other person to reciprocate."

"I'll just stick this banner in Stacy's locker; I'm sure she'll appreciate it," Harry said with a smile.

Mark uncapped the marker and handed it to Harry. "You need to lead out on this principle, so let's put this into practice. I want you to write down five people you'd like to build a stronger relationship with in your work tribe."

Harry pulled the banner closer, and, after careful consideration, wrote five names.

"What will you do?" Mark said, looking over Harry's shoulder as he read through the list.

"I guess the first thing I need to do is learn about these people and find out about their needs," Harry replied. "Then, when I get the chance, I'll try and serve those needs."

"Right," Mark said, "but always remember that although learn, serve, grow is a process, it isn't an equation that produces a predictable result." Mark pointed through the window to where different trees, bushes, and flowers edged the sides of the patio. "You must teach your tribe members to see relationships as seeds they plant and nurture. They need to understand that it's not until after the plant matures that they will find out whether they planted a vegetable, a flower, or a tree. The learn, serve, grow cycle is designed to help you form a *relationship*—not a specific outcome."

**POOLS
(Heat)**

Fish Profile

Designed Emotion

Outside Current

Effective Pull

Connects Participants

Name

Duplicatable

10.
Fish Village

Listen to the sound of the river, and you will get a trout.
—Irish Proverb

"That completes the principle arm of the fire triangle," Mark announced.

A bell rang, and the hallways flooded with students headed for their next classes. As Harry watched, the scene slowly began to blur like a camera going out of focus. Then, feeling like he was waking from a long and restful sleep, Harry opened his eyes to find himself sitting next to Patrick, floating down a river in a large wooden rowboat.

As he tried to get his bearings, Harry saw a woman materialize in front of him. She looked as surprised as he did, but when she caught sight of Patrick, she shrieked with delight. The giant hug she gave him nearly capsized the boat.

"Patrick!" she exclaimed as she released him. "I am so glad to see you! I haven't been able to concentrate on anything since I got your message this morning."

Patrick took the woman's hands in his and looked her over.

"Maggie, my darling! Look at you, all shined up like a penny!" he exclaimed.

Maggie glanced down at her fishing vest and chuckled appreciatively. "Still spouting the blarney, I see." She then turned to Harry. "And you must be Harry. I imagine you're wondering which way is up these days."

"That way, right?" Harry said, pointing to the river.

"Exactly," Maggie replied. "For weeks after my training I was positively paranoid another 'expert' was going to pop up, armed with my next lesson." She rolled her large blue eyes. "And look at me now—one of them."

"Do you work for Fish Village?" Harry asked, noticing the resort's name on the cap she wore.

Fish Village had earned the nickname the "Fisherman's Mecca," because of its reputation for drawing fishermen from all parts of the globe. Harry had friends who'd recently stayed there and couldn't stop talking about it.

Patrick looked amused. "Maggie's the proprietress, lad."

Maggie smiled, a little embarrassed, but affirmed that she was indeed the owner.

"It isn't something I've always been proud of," she admitted. "There was a time, right before I met Patrick, that I would've given Fish Village to anyone who would've taken it. And good riddance to it, as far as I was concerned, so long as I could walk away and never look back."

"I can relate," Harry said, thinking of all the times he'd considered putting Dillon-Parker on the auction block. "How did you turn it around?"

"I decided to tribe," Maggie said simply. "Instead of viewing my guests as clients I was selling to, I saw them as a group of people who were as passionate about fishing as I was. I used the secrets of tribalry to build them into a club tribe, using their devotion to fishing to connect them with each other."

As Harry pondered this, the soft breeze sent a shiver through the aspen trees lining the banks of the river. The rushing sound of the river and the warm wood against his skin made him feel strangely relaxed, like a cat basking in the sunlight. He tipped his head back and looked at the sky above them.

"I think I'm going to like this field trip," he announced.

"'Tis a fine day, to be sure, but the lesson isn't up there. It's down here," Patrick said, pointing to the river.

Under the reflection of the trees and mountains, Harry saw flashes of movement in the water. "Look at those fish," Harry exclaimed as he moved to his knees to get a closer look. "They're huge!"

The water rippled and flowed over the fish, prisms of color flashing out as their silver scales caught the sunlight.

Maneuvering herself to sit beside Harry, Maggie asked, "What do you notice about the way they're positioning themselves in the water?" she asked.

"They're all facing upstream," he said, surprised. "I always thought fish swam downstream, with the current, but they're keeping a steady position."

Patrick nodded. "Their survival depends on what they can catch floatin' toward them, but fightin' the current 'tis bitter, hard work, and a fish can be standin' it for only so long."

"It looks effortless from here," Harry said, still studying the fish.

Their fins flowed sinuously back and forth, never seeming to increase or decrease in speed. Harry noticed that even though he could see a large number of fish, they weren't in groups or schools. They were alone.

When he asked Maggie about this, she explained that the speed of the current kept them separated.

"That isn't always the case. Let's check out a few of our best fishing spots," she said.

Maggie grabbed the paddles and began rowing downstream, her capable hands pulling the oars through the water like she'd been born doing it. Navigating the boat toward a stretch of water tinged with a subtle green hue, she brought the boat alongside the trunk of a fallen tree.

"Listen, Harry. What do you hear?"

Harry listened. "It's quiet. You can barely hear the current."

Looking down into the still water, he saw that it was teaming with fish.

"There are pockets like this all along the river," Maggie explained. "They're created when something—a rock, a tree, or a bend in the river—slows the flow of the current. When a fish needs a break from fighting the current, it will seek shelter in a pool like this one."

She slowly navigated the boat around the outside edge of the pool and pointed out a large fish whose scales bulged around its belly. "For instance, do you see that fat trout in the middle? For the last three weeks that crazy guy has been swimming in this pool at exactly the same place and time."

"You've lost me. What does it have to do with building my tribe?" Harry asked, confused.

Suddenly, his stomach dropped like he'd just blasted off in a rocket. The next thing he knew, Harry was standing on a rooftop edge, watching the river below him transform into a city street crammed with rush-hour traffic. Looking down the hundred-story drop, Harry's knees buckled and he pitched forward. Two pairs of hands shot out and pulled him backward. Maggie and Patrick guided Harry off the ledge and onto the roof, hovering over him anxiously.

"Just a 'wee' bit of warning—that's all I ask," Harry said, lifting his head to glare at Patrick.

"I beg your pardon, lad. We didn't mean to give you a start," Patrick said, sounding contrite.

Patrick waited until Harry's breathing evened out before asking him if he was ready to continue. Harry nodded and stood up.

"Well, then, I'd like you to look over this fair city and tell me what you see," Patrick said.

Harry inched his way over to the ledge and gazed at the scene below. "It's New York. I can tell by the skyline. There's the Brooklyn Bridge," he said, pointing out the familiar structure. He observed the people rushing along the sidewalks and across the street. "It looks like everyone's heading for work."

"Now, think back to the river . . . do you see any similarities?" Maggie asked.

As Harry looked out over the city again, the scene morphed before his eyes. The street wound and twisted like the river, a dull roar rising from it like the sound of whitewater rapids. The yellow, silver, and blue cars transformed into fish, moving in and out of the current, fighting for survival. The people on the sidewalks and those filling the offices in the adjacent buildings transformed into fish as well, locked in the struggle to get ahead.

"I get it," Harry said slowly. "The current . . . and the fish."

"Do you be seeing how the speed of the current keeps them separated?" Patrick asked.

Harry nodded. The scenario was all too familiar.

"Just like fish, your tribe members spend the majority of their day fighting for survival in the current," Maggie explained, her gaze sweeping over the congested streets, crowded sidewalks, and office buildings below them. "The current represents task-oriented, results-driven work environments where production and efficiency are the primary drivers."

That about sums up my entire life, Harry thought.

"Your tribe members tend to spend most of their time in the current, doing the 'work.' They're selling, marketing, ordering, managing staff, paying the bills, and juggling a million other things."

Maggie pointed to the building across the way. Harry could see people hurrying between the cubicles with bulging files in their hands. Others were either talking on their phones or glued to their computer screens, typing furiously.

"Can you see how difficult it is for your tribe to build relationships with each other when they're inside the current?" Maggie asked. "Interrupt people when they're entrenched in their task-driven mindset, and they're sure to see you as an irritation or even worse. In contrast, a correctly designed pool is the perfect environment for relationship building."

As Harry remembered the fish he'd seen swimming lazily through the pool, he suddenly realized he couldn't remember the last time he'd really relaxed and connected with his work tribe.

"Pools are experiences that remove a person from their 'work mindset,' allowing them to reconnect with the people around them," Maggie said. "People in the current who wouldn't give you the time of day quickly transform inside the relaxed pace of a pool."

The street slowly took on a bluish hue as the scene began to shift. Harry tried to grab on to the ledge, but it evaporated beneath his fingers, and he dropped through space again.

Frantically trying to break his fall, he reached out and caught something solid. Curling his fingers around it, he opened his eyes and found himself clutching the side of the boat.

"They've got to build something like this at an amusement park," Harry said breathlessly, his heart still thudding against his ribs. "It would make millions."

"We try to keep you on your toes," Patrick replied with a modest shrug of his shoulders.

Maggie unzipped a pocket on her fishing vest. "Do you have the fire triangle Afu gave you?"

Harry quickly retrieved the small golden object from his pocket and showed it to Maggie. The second side of the triangle ignited; a flame burning the word "Pools" into it.

"The second arm of tribalry is the practice of building pools. Just as heat gives the first spark of life to the fire, a true pool is where relationships ignite. The bond that is created when people experience meaningful connection inside a pool is one of the most magical secrets of building connection and community," Maggie said.

Patrick then nudged Harry and pointed to the surface of the water. "Take a gander at that wee little fish. What a sad fellow he is."

Pocketing the triangle, Harry looked down into the water to see a silver fish straining desperately against the current. It gradually slowed down, out of what appeared to be pure exhaustion, and was carried downstream several feet. While trying to maintain its position, the fish kept his mouth wide open, darting to catch anything coming down the river.

Harry felt a sudden rush of pity for the fish. "That fish is pretty hard-core. Why doesn't he swim into that pool?" he said, pointing to where several large gray boulders had slowed the current. "He's never going to survive at this rate."

"His name is Harry Green," Maggie replied. "He works fourteen-hour days, then heads home to his family tribe, eats and sleeps, and plunges back into the current again."

Harry stared down at the fish. He felt a prickle run down the back of his neck as he noticed an odd resemblance.

"We're not saying you shouldn't be spending time in the current doing the work of your business," Patrick continued before Harry could protest, "but to be a strong tribe leader, you must also swim in pools."

The little silver fish continued to swim frantically against the current but was swept farther and farther downstream.

"I do feel like that fish most of the time," Harry admitted. "It seems the harder I fight, the further I get behind."

11.

Dam It

May the holes in your net be no larger than the fish in it.

—Irish Blessing

They quietly watched the fish until it disappeared from view. A birdcall broke the silence, its sound echoing off the jagged mountain cliffs.

Maggie reached into one of her pockets and pulled out a laminated card in the shape of a fish. "There are seven ingredients needed to build an effective pool."

She handed Harry the card:

Build a Pool

1. Fish Profile: Who is it for?

2. Designed Emotion: How will it make them feel?

3. Outside the Current: Is it in a non-task-centered environment?

4. Effective Pull: Is the experience compelling?

5. Connects Participants: Is there facilitated interaction?

6. Name: Does it have a memorable name?

7. Duplictable: Can it be repeated?

Maggie pointed to the first ingredient. "The first thing you need to do when building a pool is to decide who you are building it for. The answers to the seven questions will be different, depending on what kind of 'fish' will be there."

Handing Harry a pencil, Maggie asked Harry to turn over the card and identify tribe gatherings he'd attended in the last year. Harry considered this and realized each of his tribes had had at least one event:

Work tribe: Monthly birthday lunch

Family tribe: Family reunion at a beach house

Sports tribe: Softball tournament

Church tribe: Nativity dinner and program

Neighborhood tribe: Annual hotdog roast and bonfire

Association tribe: Design conference

Non-Profit tribe: Animal rescue fundraiser

Business School tribe: Alumni networking breakfast

"So, all these are pools?" Harry asked.

"Maybe," Maggie responded. "Look at the ingredients. Do any of the events you listed have all seven?"

Harry used the card as a checklist to evaluate the gatherings.

"No," he finally responded. "Some of them have a couple ingredients, but they are all missing at least two or three."

"That is usually the case. True pools are a rare commodity," Maggie explained.

She then pointed out a slackening in the current of the river's sparkling, snakelike path, and traced it back to its source: a large mound of sticks and mud. A beaver suddenly appeared on top of the dam, carrying a stick between its teeth, its fur matted down with water.

"A beaver," Harry said. "It always amazes me how animals can build things like that."

He watched the beaver drop the stick on the dam, then crawl down the outside of it and plunge back into the river.

"When established events don't meet the requirements for a pool, tribe leaders need to think like a beaver and build their own," Maggie explained. "We call it the 'Dam It' principle. Following the recipe for a pool, tribe leaders can either use the pool ingredients to redesign an existing pool or create something entirely new."

"Got it," Harry said. "What's next?"

"Designed emotion is the second secret of true pool builders," Patrick said, pointing to the next ingredient. "You must first be deciding the mood you're wanting to create for each particular pool, then carefully craft an environment fosterin' those emotions. Pool builders are masters at packagin' their pools so that even the most contrary lads and lasses look forward to swimmin' in them," Patrick explained. "They know 'tis not the event itself that creates the desire to return, but the memory of the emotion."

Thinking back to the places he loved to be—whether it was at the football stadium or the long stretch of beach where his family sometimes spent Saturday afternoons—Harry agreed that it was the feelings these places created that drew him back again.

"I think I understand," Harry said. "What's next?"

"We've already talked about how a pool needs to be outside the current to be effective, but it must also have enough 'pull' to draw people in. That's why it's so important to know your fish profile—because you have to create a compelling experience that your tribe members are naturally attracted to," Maggie explained.

"That's true," Harry agreed. "I'm invited to events all the time, but I only go to the ones that sound like they'll be worth my time."

"Many people intuitively understand that a pool must be both outside the current and have effective pull," Maggie told Harry. "But it's the next ingredient that's most often overlooked—which is a huge mistake, because facilitating interaction between the participants is the whole point of a pool."

Maggie asked Harry if he'd ever attended an event that was outside the current and had effective pull but where he didn't build any new relationships. An example instantly popped into his mind. The design conference he'd recently attended had dynamic speakers and relevant topics, but the participants had been herded from one venue to the next without any opportunities to interact. Harry didn't connect with a single person during the entire two-day event.

"They could've taken that experience from average to exceptional simply by facilitating some relationship building," Maggie said, shaking her head.

Remembering how isolated he'd felt during the conference, Harry had to agree with her.

"The next ingredient is to give your pool a name," Maggie said. "Patrick, this is one of your favorites. Why don't you take this one?"

"I'd be pleased to," Patrick responded. "You see, Harry, most lads and lasses will spend loads of time creating the perfect pool, then, like they have heads full of cider, select its name as an afterthought. It destroys the craft not to do it properly!"

Patrick became so passionate that the boat nearly capsized a second time. He apologized as he helped steady the boat but carried on with his point. "Answer me this. Have you ever decided not to attend a 'seminar,' a 'networking session,' or—saints forbid—a 'lecture'?"

"Of course. That is, unless I needed a good nap," Harry replied dryly.

"You see how naming the pool plays a part in giving it effective pull?" Patrick asked.

"The last ingredient is making the pool duplicatable," Maggie said. "Although this isn't always possible, it is the goal. Tell me, why would you want to build a pool you can hold more than once?"

Harry gazed meditatively over the river.

"Relationships need time to develop," he finally said. "Interacting with a person one time isn't going to build a very strong relationship. Plus, it may take a couple of times in the same pool before I trust that the experience is worth my time."

"We have a sayin' in Ireland: 'The mason who strikes often is better than the one who strikes too hard,'" Patrick agreed.

"Have you noticed how he seems to have a proverb for every situation?" Maggie asked. "I've been wondering for years if they're real or if he just makes them up."

"Right, now that be a trade secret, lass," Patrick replied with a wink.

Maggie steered the boat to a large inlet on the river, and around the bend they saw a bustling pier with all shapes and sizes of boats docked alongside it. Above the pier, nestled among a forest of pines and aspens, stood an enormous, rough-hewn lodge. The words "Fish Village" were engraved on the center of the rock wall sign in front of the lodge, and a waterfall cascaded over bronze fish sculptures in the pool below it. Harry drew in his breath; he hadn't realized he might get the chance to visit the luxurious resort.

Maggie guided the boat toward the dock and jumped out. She used a stout gray rope to secure the boat to a pillar.

"I guess this is good-bye," she said, obviously reluctant to leave. "I need to take care of the finishing touches for our annual Fattest Fish Competition. It's our largest pool of the year, and if I don't get back soon, my staff will probably throw me in the river. But I'll be seeing you both again soon enough," she finished, brightening at the thought.

"Thank you, Maggie," Harry said. "For everything."

"It was my pleasure," Maggie replied. Then she added in a confidential whisper, "For future reference, it's much more fun being on this side of the training."

She waved good-bye and was soon swallowed up by the thick pine trees lining the path. Patrick and Harry exited the boat and sat on the long wooden dock, enjoying the sunshine.

"Why don't we take a look about," Patrick suggested.

Within minutes they were standing inside the front lobby of Fish Village. Harry's attention was immediately drawn to two large photographs hung carefully above the stone fireplace. One picture showed two men proudly holding up a prize trout. The other picture captured three guests sprawled out on the bank of the river, their poles hanging over the water and their hats pulled over their eyes.

Harry and Patrick passed by the Fish Village restaurant, spa, and indoor convention space before stepping out onto a balcony overlooking the enormous patio skirting the back side of the resort. Below them dozens of people were sitting around tables, dressed in hats and fishing vests. The place felt alive with energy as the group talked and laughed, and the smell of fresh salmon sizzling on the grill made Harry's mouth water.

Maggie stepped up to a small stage with the wilderness as her backdrop. "Welcome to Fish Village's Semi-Annual Fattest Fish Competition," she proclaimed after quieting the group down.

She explained that they were sitting with their assigned team. The competition would begin soon and each team was required to report back with their catches no later than eight o'clock that night.

"As you all know, the team that brings in the fattest fish wins a weekend stay at Fish Village and a $5,000 shopping spree at the store."

There was cheering and heckling from the audience; their enthusiasm was infectious.

"But before I turn you loose," Maggie continued, "we're giving you time to get to know your team. Each of you take five minutes to introduce yourself and share a memorable fishing experience."

Maggie rang an old cowbell, and one person at each table began talking while the others listened.

"This is her pool?" Harry asked, impressed.

"Aye, lad. There are thousands of grand places to fish the world over, so what would make someone choose Fish Village over another spot?"

"The chance to be part of a tribe of people who are just as passionate about something as you are," Harry replied.

"And does this experience have all seven ingredients of a pool?" Patrick asked.

Harry thought back to Maggie's criteria. The resort was outside the current, and the experience obviously had enough pull. It also had a memorable name and designed emotion, and she'd mentioned it was a semi-annual event, so it was duplicatable.

Harry ticked off each ingredient on his fingers as he identified them. "Wait. I'm forgetting one," he said, pulling out his card to check himself. "Connect the participants!"

Patrick nodded. "Right. Did you notice how Maggie facilitated interaction by putting people in teams and startin' a conversation? That is the secret of her success. When you structure an experience that helps people to connect and to build relationships with other tribe members, they will always come back to swim again."

PLATFORM
(OXYGEN)

tribalry.com

12.
Tribe Fire

The fat is not to be had without the labor.

—Irish Proverb

Harry found himself sitting at his desk, the chimes from the hallway clock signaling the passing of another hour. Gradually they were replaced by the soft patter of raindrops falling on the slate roof of his home. Going to the window, Harry nudged it open and inhaled deeply.

"If I'm going to turn this thing around, I need to unify my tribe," he murmured to himself, so absorbed in his thoughts that he barely registered the loud crack of thunder above him. "But how am I supposed to connect with my tribe every day and still finish everything else I'm responsible for? I just can't see how this is practical."

He gripped the window ledge in frustration. It felt as though he were living thousands of years ago, watching lightning strike for the first time. He could see the power of tribes, but he couldn't harness it.

A web of lightning lit up the dark street, and Harry thought he saw the outline of a man scurrying up the walkway, but when a second flash illuminated the landscape, no one was there.

"*Ja*, you need a system!" a voice boomed out behind him.

Harry's heart jumped. He whirled around to see a pair of wire-rimmed glasses suspended in midair. Gradually a face appeared, along with a body wearing a graphic T-shirt, jeans, and bright orange sneakers.

The man came forward and shook Harry's hand. "*Guten Tag*. I am Newton Schwartz," he said. Then, noticing Harry's expression, he added, "It seems I have alarmed you. For this I am sorry."

"I really should be used to it by now," Harry responded.

Newton explained that his training session would be held in the adjoining storage room and motioned for Harry to follow him. As Harry entered the room, he discovered two large boxes sitting on the floor, and rigging set up at the top of each wall. Newton pushed a button, and two large screens descended, locking into place on the floor below.

"It will take some time for the system to power up. Since we have a moment, perhaps you will allow me to share a story about myself?" Newton asked.

"I'd like that," Harry replied, intensely curious about his newest trainer.

"Many years ago, I went home to tell my mother I had fallen in love and was going to marry. I told her I would bring home three women, and she should guess which one I had chosen for my bride. So the next day, I sit the women down on the couch, and they began to talk and visit. When I asked which woman she thought I would marry, she chose the one in the middle. '*Fantastisch*, Mama!' I said, 'How did you know?' and she replied, 'I do not like her.'"

Laughter shook Newton's entire body. He finally had to remove his glasses to wipe the tears streaming from his eyes. Harry laughed heartily as well, though more at Newton's reaction than at the joke itself.

"How are you going to tie that in to the training?" Harry finally asked, trying to remember the last time he'd really laughed like that.

"Not everything is about the training, Harry," Newton said, shaking his head in amusement. "When building relationships, business is often the last thing you discuss."

Both screens now glowed with a warm yellow light. "They are ready," Newton announced.

Newton tapped his tablet, and immediately a live feed of Afu's village appeared on both screens.

Twilight had just fallen, Drumbeats filled the air and the light from numerous tiki torches bobbed up and down as tribe members arrived from all directions. As the tribe congregated around the large fire at the center of the village, the air hummed with conversation and fits of laughter.

When Afu stood, the group hushed and gave him their attention. He began by sharing a story about his experience as a young wayfinder. During a terrible famine, he and his small team evacuated the entire tribe to a neighboring island. The voyage across hundreds of miles of open ocean had been treacherous, and he had almost lost his life several times. Harry found himself completely absorbed in the story and felt a strong wave of relief when it ended happily.

Afu then reminded the group of the possibility of tropical storms hitting the island that summer and asked the tribe for ideas on how they could prepare their huts, animals, and food supplies. The question sparked a lively discussion that ended with several tribe members being assigned specific responsibilities.

Without encouragement, several other tribe members then began sharing their stories. After a time, the stories turned into questions, with the wiser tribe members counseling the less experienced. The bond around the campfire was tangible, and in a flash of insight, Harry realized that in some ways these people were much wealthier than he was. He had literally been starving for something he didn't even know existed.

Newton tapped his tablet, and the screens went dark.

When he saw Harry's expression, Newton explained, "Meaningful connection is a basic human need, Harry. It acts as a magnet, drawing our tribe members back over and over again."

"They gather like that every night?" Harry asked.

"A simpler time," Newton confirmed with a nod. "This is Afu's system for maintaining relationships on a daily basis, but your world has no tribe fire. You are busy, busy; always busy. But remember, if we make no time for relationships, they will eventually die. So my question is this: How much time could an average member of your tribe spend connecting each day?"

"We could probably find an extra ten to fifteen minutes a day," Harry said.

"Produce your fire triangle, if you please," Newton directed.

Fishing the golden triangle out of his pocket, Harry held it out to Newton. The third side of the triangle lit up, and the word "Platform" blazed across its surface.

"Platform is the final secret of tribalry and the third arm of the fire triangle," Newton stated. "Without oxygen the flame will quickly go out. Without a place where tribe members can turn intermittent tribe communication into consistent tribe collaboration, the tribe relationships will weaken over time."

The screens powered up again, now displaying the tribalry.com login page. Newton gave Harry a user name and password, and the screens filled with familiar faces.

"This is the Dillon-Parker tribe," Harry said, looking at the screen in surprise. "Is this my platform?"

"*Ja!* For the modern tribe leader, the foundation has created a virtual tribe fire patterned after Afu's real-life version."

"Any tribe leader?" Harry asked.

"Anyone that is certified. Each of your trainers uses this online platform to communicate with their tribes—I use it for my tech tribe, Angela uses it for her medical association tribe, Maggie uses it for her fishing tribe, Kris uses is for his non-profit tribe, Mark uses it for his singles' tribe, Cordelia uses it for her homeschooling tribe. It provides each of us a private platform to use the power of stories, questions, and discussion to keep our tribe connected— just like Afu did. Let us take a few minutes and learn about one of your tribe members. Please note the time."

Harry checked his watch, then used Newton's tablet to begin navigating the software. He clicked on the button labeled "Stories." When he did, a large number of leather books filled the screen, each with a colorful photograph imbedded in its surface. Harry clicked on a book displaying a small group of hunters inside a wooded grove. Inside the book, Harry discovered a story submitted by Marta, his senior web designer.

After reading about a family hunting trip with her dad and three brothers, Harry commented, "That's hilarious! I would never have guessed that in a million years. I can't even imagine her shooting a gun."

"You see, in sixty seconds you have learned something important about a member of your tribe. You now have something to talk of, questions to ask, a way to relate."

Marta's picture suddenly disappeared. "Hey, what happened to her?"

"Do not worry. She will be back later. Now is the time to find a tribe member to serve."

Newton then asked Harry to click on the button labeled "Questions." When he did, a photo of Bruce Ballard from Human Resources appeared. Bruce was requesting ideas for improving the annual Dillon-Parker awards celebration.

"Thanks to Maggie, I can definitely help Bruce with this one." Harry said.

Harry outlined the ingredients of a pool and asked Bruce to schedule a meeting with him to explain them further.

Newton asked Harry to check the time on his watch.

"Five minutes," Harry said, surprised.

"Tell me this: Did taking a few minutes to 'sit around' your tribe fire make a difference?" Newton asked.

Harry looked at the images of Marta and Bruce and slowly nodded. He did feel more connected to both of them.

"As you can see, this powerful tool helps even the busiest of people participate and become effective members of your tribe—especially if you remember one rule."

"What is that?" Harry asked, his curiosity piqued.

"When it comes to building your platform, you must remember the old saying that a fish stinks from the head down. The tribalry platform only works when a tribe leader fully engages. If you lead, they will follow."

"Point taken," Harry said, clicking on the option labeled "Create Story" and selecting the topic "Share one of your favorite outdoor experiences." Harry wrote the story of a memorable climbing experience in the Tetons and submitted it.

Harry began to imagine what his work tribe would be like if they really knew each other and were constantly looking for ways to serve each other. It would certainly be different, that's for sure, but better . . . way better.

Harry's thoughts turned back to Afu's tribe and their nightly tribe fires. *That level of connection and collaboration is exactly what I want and precisely what the company needs to be successful. This is going to be good.*

Droplets of rain began to pound more heavily against the roof, and another lightning pattern lit up the night sky.

Newton moved over to the window and invited Harry to join him. "You have been unable to tap into the power of relationships—just as the ancients were unable to capture lightning. This platform will give your tribe the ability to easily and effectively connect on a daily basis."

Another bolt of lightning struck.

"You now have the power to harness your lightning," Newton concluded.

13.
Two Roads

The longest road out is the shortest road home.

—Irish Proverb

A roll of thunder shook the house, and Harry suddenly found himself standing beside Patrick on a dirt road. Ten feet ahead, the path forked.

"Why do I feel like I just landed in a Robert Frost poem?" Harry asked, his gaze shifting between the two paths.

Strangely familiar, the one to the right wound its way along a tree-lined slope and disappeared into a valley of rolling green hills, while the narrow, brick-paved path on the left snaked up a steep mountain incline, with no indication of what lay beyond.

"Which one do I take?" he asked.

"I knew a young lass named Alice who once asked that same question of a cat," Patrick said conversationally, climbing on one of the railings of the wooden fence lining the road.

Harry rolled his eyes. "It didn't happen to be a Cheshire cat, did it?"

"Aye, it was!" Patrick exclaimed, startled. "Have you met Miss Alice?"

Harry just shook his head.

"No? Well, the way she tells it, when she asked the cat which path she should be takin', he said that depended entirely on where she was wantin' to end up. Miss Alice told him she didn't much care so long as she arrived somewhere."

"And what did the cat say?" Harry asked, climbing up beside Patrick, intrigued in spite of himself.

Patrick inspected his fingernails closely. "He told Miss Alice that if she didn't care where she ended up, it didn't much matter which way she went."

Harry gave Patrick a long look. "Are you asking me where I want to end up? What are my choices?"

"The road yonder is your first choice," Patrick said pointing down the shady pathway winding through a lush valley.

Harry felt a strange sense of nostalgia as he looked down the lane. It was as though he had arrived at this intersection a thousand times before, and this was the path he'd always taken.

"It looks so familiar," he told Patrick.

"That's because you've been down that path already," Patrick replied, confirming Harry's suspicions. "That's the road to the coliseum."

Harry ventured over to the trailhead of the second path. "And this one?" he asked, his gaze lingering on the spot where the steep brick pathway disappeared into the mountainside.

Patrick jumped off the fence and went to stand beside Harry. "If you've a mind to climb it, that would be the path to Tribalry Summit, but I'll be warning you now, 'tis the longer, more demanding path."

It was obvious to Harry why he had always chosen the first road. One promised a predictable walk, while the other guaranteed an intense climb.

Patrick looked as serious as Harry had ever seen him. "We're at the beginnin' again. Now that you understand tribes—their costs and blessings—the time has come for you to make a true choice. There'll be no contract this time—'tis a commitment you make to yourself."

Patrick opened his hands to indicate the different options.

"Make no mistake about it, these roads are real. You can stay with what you know and follow the path to the coliseum, hoping to become a champion gladiator by fighting your way to survival, or you can decide to tribe and begin gathering the relationships that'll sustain you through a lifetime."

Harry bit his lip as he looked back and forth between the two roads, but deep down he knew he'd already made his decision. He took the left fork and began climbing up the mountainous path.

"I'll be waitin' for you at the top," Patrick called out, waving him on.

Although Harry knew he'd made the right decision, he began to wonder if he had the stamina to reach the top. His work schedule hadn't allowed for much in the way of exercise the last couple years, and he was paying a serious price for it now.

The climb was steep from the start, stretching ever upward, and the loose rocks, which had eventually replaced the brick path, shifted under his feet and slowed his progress. In some places, the path narrowed so sharply that Harry struggled to find footholds and had to cling to roots and small bushes just to stay upright.

As the sun beat down hotter and hotter, his breathing became labored, and a fierce burning sensation spread throughout his chest. At the crest of the first hill, he saw an enormous peak looming in front of him, the path running a jagged progression up the mountain. As Harry stared up at it, he saw the silhouettes of other people farther along the path and realized there were others making the same journey.

The path then began alternating between sharp, rocky ledges—where the trees bent almost in half as they struggled to remain parallel to the mountainside—and occasional flat stretches through sunken mountain meadows. Harry took several detours off the beaten path to rest his feet in the thick mountain grass.

Near the peak, he had to navigate fields of boulders and stretches of glacier ice before approaching the final climb to the summit. Harry wasn't sure how many hours had passed, but he was pretty sure his legs couldn't hold out much longer. Using his last ounce of energy, he crested the final ridge, and a spectacular vista burst before him.

Harry caught his breath in wonder as he lowered his exhausted body to a flat stone ledge at the top, his gaze never leaving the valley below. From this high up, he could visually trace the route of the first path. "It's just a big circle! The path doesn't go anywhere but back to the coliseum."

He didn't hear Patrick come up behind him but wasn't surprised to hear his voice.

"Where else would daily battles against other people lead?" Patrick said as he took a seat next to Harry.

"To more daily battles," Harry answered, feeling like he was finally beginning to really understand. He leaned back on his elbows and absently stared at the large formations of clouds congregating along the skyline. "I have to admit, in the beginning, battling in the coliseum was kind of a rush. You really do believe if you just get in there and fight hard enough, you'll eventually find a way to win."

A blast of trumpets rang out from a huge stone structure in the valley, and the throbbing drumbeats signaled that the games were about to begin. Patrick removed a pair of binoculars that hung around his neck and handed them to Harry. Focusing them on the playing field, Harry watched as a gladiator slowly limped to the center of the field and raised his sword with great effort. The crowd responded with a deafening roar.

Harry felt deep empathy mixed with frustration as he watched the battle begin. Slaves appeared on opposite sides of the arena, pulling on the leashes of two snarling wolves. As they released the wolves, the crowd let out a scream of approval. The animals began to circle the gladiator until one finally attacked.

"Why is he fighting wolves?" Harry asked. "Where are the other gladiators?"

"'Tis not only competitors who kill companies," Patrick replied. "That particular lad happens to be battling financial reversals from product defects, but there are a thousand different kinds of wolves that can destroy an organization."

Harry watched the gladiator strike one wolf down, but behind him, the other one lunged, skimming the gladiator's side with its sharp teeth as the gladiator rolled out of its reach and sprang back to his feet. As the animal charged forward, the gladiator picked up a javelin from the ground and hurled it into the face of the beast. The wolf went down in a cloud of dust, sending the crowd into a frenzy as they chanted the gladiator's name.

"Another gladiator hailed as a hero," Patrick observed, his face tense.

"Until tomorrow," Harry responded grimly.

Patrick sat silently, his face working to contain the emotions he was feeling. "I'm sick of the sight, though it be familiar enough," he said. "These eager lads and lasses walk into the arena and try to do it all by themselves. Whether they live or die, it makes no difference to the crowd; they'll scream just as loud when the wolves win."

A cheer went up from the coliseum as another gladiator was struck down.

"And who says the tribalry path is harder?" Harry wondered.

Picking up the thread of his story where he'd left off earlier in the evening, Patrick said, "I arrived on the shores of this country starving and penniless. The moment my feet touched American soil, I began my search for work. In the beginnin', I could only get factory work, makin' wages that barely kept us alive. 'Twas a bitter thing for me to have rescued my family from famine only to see them live in squalor. It put me into quite a temper, I can tell you that. But I was determined to get ahead, and soon enough I was a full-fledged gladiator, fightin' tooth and nail in the coliseum."

As he spoke, Patrick's face took on a hard expression Harry had never seen before. At that moment, he could picture him waging his battle against his opponents, no matter who he hurt in the process.

"Through grit and hard work, I eventually scrimped enough to begin a small manufacturin' establishment of my own," he continued. "A prize-winnin' fighter in the price-and-performance wars. Your work tribe looks like a thrivin' metropolis compared to the depths mine had sunk to. People were emigratin' out of it like 'twas hell itself!" Patrick said, shaking his head at the memory.

"Then I met your great-great-grandfather, and things began to change. I was a supplier for his small shop and was critical of the way he ran his business and told Molly he was a sentimental fool. But like everyone else who knew George, he eventually won me over. Sure, he was one of the rare ones—a lad as genuinely interested in the success of others as he was in his own. As time went on, instead of going bankrupt, as I expected, his business began to prosper. After watchin' this for a time, I finally worked up the courage to ask him about it."

Harry could picture the two men sitting together by the fire as George explained the secrets of tribalry to Patrick.

"From that day on, we began buildin' our tribes together, and it didn't take us long to realize that there wasn't a thing in the world we couldn't accomplish with the help of others. George sold his shop to join me as my partner, and within ten years our team of broken-down

Irish immigrants had become one of the largest workforces in America by looking out for each other's interests—provin' you didn't have to beat down your employees, competitors, and clients to make a profit."

Harry had studied enough about their company to know the rest of the story. They had been successful beyond belief.

Patrick interrupted his thoughts. "Now, lad, I've a few important questions to ask you."

"You're not going to dump me back into the coliseum if I answer them wrong, are you?" Harry asked, only half joking.

"Don't worry, lad. You're sure to be knowing the answers," Patrick reassured him. "What is the definition of tribalry?"

"The art of building connection and community."

Patrick nodded, "What is the difference between a tribe leader and a gladiator?" Patrick asked.

Harry took plenty of time to gather his thoughts, replaying the lessons of the evening in his mind.

"Gladiators make self-preservation their primary concern and personal victory their highest ambition. Tribe leaders make the success of their tribe members their highest priority."

"So what will be your purpose as a tribe leader—as the leader of your company?" Patrick asked.

Harry scanned the distant cities on the horizon.

"Tribe leaders train and motivate their tribe members to learn about and serve each other through implementing principles, pools, and the platform inside their tribes," he finally responded.

"And that's the secret, lad. Success isn't complicated, and it isn't about money. Real success is reserved for the rare few who care enough to build unified tribes and who give back to the people who belong to them."

It was as if all the lessons had found their position and locked perfectly into place.

"So, we've reached the end?" Harry asked.

"Aye, but 'tis a journey you'll have to be making over and over again," Patrick warned. He walked to the ledge and looked down at the path Harry had just climbed. "Every step of your journey to Tribalry Summit represented one of the actions of a tribe leader. It may be buildin' a relationship 'just because,' holdin' an effective pool, or creatin' a virtual tribe fire as a gathering place. Each of these things will take effort; they will take discipline."

Harry stood beside Patrick and looked down at the path as well. Although it was precarious, and climbing it had required all his strength, at least it wasn't infested with wild animals or gladiators trying to tear him apart.

"The climb wasn't easy," Harry said slowly. "I thought about turning back a couple of times, but now, looking at it from this perspective, I'm glad I was investing my effort in something meaningful instead of wasting my resources running in circles."

Patrick gave a quick nod of approval. "By deciding to tribe, you'll increase in all the areas that a person can be wealthy—in your business, your family, your community, and your friendships."

Harry's gaze swept across the coliseum one last time.

"I've seen enough," he said, turning away from the cliff's edge.

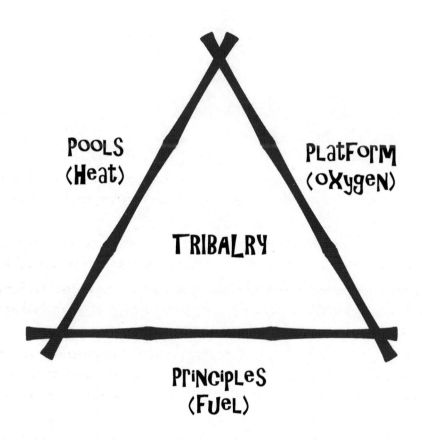

14.
Fire 2.0

'Tis afterwards that everything is understood.

—Irish Proverb

Without warning, their location changed again. Patrick and Harry stood before a large brick mansion. Warm yellow light spilled from its diamond-paned windows onto the lush green lawn below.

"Welcome back to my home, Harry," Patrick said, then opened the front door. As Harry followed him into a darkened entryway, the lights flipped on, and voices yelled out, "Surprise!"

Harry had never been to a surprise party before, least of all one thrown for him. Surrounded by his new friends, he couldn't believe this many people—most of whom he'd never met before tonight—would care enough to put something like this together.

In the kitchen, Molly had prepared a feast for a king, with mouthwatering meats, mounds of fruit, and elaborate desserts. Everyone pitched in by carrying platters of food to a long mahogany table. After they took their seats, Patrick stood at the head of the table and held up a glass.

"I want to welcome all of you to Harry's graduation party. As you know, we have a traditional Irish toast for just such occasions," Patrick announced.

Everyone at the table lifted their glasses, and Harry followed suit.

"May the roof above us never fall in, and may the friends below it never fall out," Patrick said.

"Hear, hear!" everyone chorused.

The group sat down and instantly began chattering and bantering with each other. As the dinner progressed, the trainers took turns sharing their stories about Harry. He laughed right along with them, enjoying the retellings of his journey as much as they did. After they'd finished eating and cleared the dishes, the trainers returned to the table, exchanging devious looks.

"Okay, what's going on?" asked Harry, looking around suspiciously. "I can tell you guys are up to something."

Kris let out a hearty chuckle and said, "As the newest member of our foundation tribe, you now have access to our time, influence and resources. To demonstrate this, Patrick has introduced a little competition of sorts. We've all had the chance to learn a little about you tonight, and now we get the opportunity to see if we can serve you in some way."

Mark spoke up. "I'll go first," he said. "I know you have a serious cash-flow problem, and, as a last resort, you've maxed out all of your credit cards. I think I've got just the man to help. He's an outside investor who likes to take on crazy, high-risk clients like you. He'll be giving you a call."

Harry's mouth dropped open in amazement, but before he could say anything, Maggie began telling the group how she'd learned that Harry needed some advice on bankruptcy laws because a major client had recently gone under with a large invoice unpaid.

"I discussed the situation with a lawyer friend who was attending our Fattest Fish Competition, and he said he'd be happy to give you a little free advice. Bankruptcy happens to be his specialty," Maggie finished, handing Harry a card.

As Harry stared down at the card, he felt his shoulders relax for the first time in months.

Kris spoke next. "We learned your daughter has been struggling with her speech and is getting teased at school. Angela and I discussed it, and she called a couple of highly respected speech pathologists."

"I called a number of them to ask the best thing to do," Angela piped in. "I emailed you their recommendations."

Cordelia pulled out a slip of paper with two names and phone numbers scrawled on it. "I know a couple of CEOs who are looking into rebranding. Here are their names and numbers," she said, passing the paper to Harry. "I told them someone from your company would be calling them to set up a presentation."

The trainers continued to share their gifts until each had taken a turn.

Harry looked around the table in amazement. He had long since decided this wasn't a dream, but he could never have guessed things would turn out this well. "I don't know what to say."

Patrick leaned over and elbowed Harry. "The end of a feast is better than the beginnin' of a fight, eh? Tell me now, Harry Green, should I have brought all these solutions to you at the start of the evenin'?"

Harry shook his head. "Other problems would've just jumped in to take their place, and I would've been right back where I started." He looked down at Patrick gratefully. "You taught me how to fish."

Harry looked up to find that the others were leaving their seats and forming a line in the entryway.

"We have one last tradition for our graduates," Patrick explained as he ushered Harry to the hallway.

Afu moved toward Harry first and handed him an amulet embossed with flames. The words "Fire Triangle" were inscribed on its surface. "The secrets of tribalry are found in the three sides of the triangle. Bring these elements to your tribe to ignite a new kind of connection and community."

Patrick came next, handing Harry a postcard with a misty mountain peak and "Decide to Tribe" on it. Harry recognized the mountain as the peak he'd just climbed. "The Tribe5 principles be startin' with commitment. As a tribe leader, you must be exiting the coliseum and makin' the success of your tribe your primary concern."

Cordelia came forward, giving Harry a gold ring that had the words "Invisible Threads" inscribed on it.

"Tribe leaders understand that every opportunity has its root in a relationship. They know they can't live for themselves alone because their lives are connected by a thousand invisible threads." Cordelia hugged him and whispered, "Good luck, Harry."

Angela came next, placing a pair of glasses in Harry's hands. They had the words "Avoid Relationship Arrogance" printed on the frame.

"To help you see more clearly," she explained. "Tribe leaders never assume they know what people have to offer. Some of your most valuable opportunities will come from the least likely of places."

"Thanks, Angela. I'll be back if any of my symptoms flare up," Harry replied with a grateful smile.

Kris's deep laugh rang out as he stepped forward. He put his arm around Harry and handed him a gold package tied with a crimson ribbon. The attached tag read, "Develop Relationships Just Because."

"People can sense when a tribe leader's motives are genuine. Remember to build relationships 'just because' and concentrate on seeing people for who they really are."

For some reason Harry always got emotional around Kris, but he managed to get out a husky, "Thank you."

Mark came next, holding out a pot with a green shoot beginning to poke through the soil. The pot had "Learn, Serve, Grow" etched on its ceramic surface.

"Use the learn, serve, grow cycle to build lasting relationships, and be sure to let others reciprocate. And don't forget we're doing lunch on Friday," Mark added with a grin.

Maggie stepped forward and handed Harry a fishing hook with colorful lures attached to it. "Build Pools" was engraved on its surface.

"Tribe leaders are committed to helping their tribes spend less time inside fast-paced, task-centered environments. Instead, they encourage them to build meaningful connections in the slower pace of a pool." She gave Harry a hug and moved on.

Newton approached Harry and gave him a silver lightning bolt. The bolt had the word "tribalry.com" engraved on it. "As a tribe leader, you must use the platform that allows your members to regularly learn about and serve each other. If you do this, the relationships in your tribe will continue to grow over time."

The trainers then gathered around Harry to congratulate him. Talking and laughing, they gradually drifted out the front door and congregated on the porch that wrapped around the front of the house.

Evening had arrived, and the breeze was drenched with the smell of honeysuckle. Some of the trainers took a seat on the cushioned lawn chairs while others settled themselves on the thick porch railing, swinging their legs as they talked. Patrick and Harry sat down together on either side of the front step, leaning their backs against the finely carved balusters for support.

"Aligning your life with the fire triangle may be a difficult challenge, lad," Patrick said slowly. "That's the reason I wanted to bring you here—so you could see for yourself that, in the end, the sacrifice will be worth it."

Swallowing a couple of times, Harry absently gazed at the gifts the others had given him.

"How can I ever thank you?" he finally said.

Patrick smiled and put his arm around his shoulders. "I believe you just did, lad. You're a credit to your great-great-grandfather, and I've a feelin' that you're goin' to be just like him. Now, 'tis time you finally got some rest."

Harry heard the muffled clanging of the grandfather clock inside the mansion. His eyelids grew heavy, and the porch lights blurred and eventually faded into darkness. The next thing he knew, his right cheek was pressed against something smooth and hard. Reluctantly opening his eyes, Harry gazed down at the dark wood grain of his desk. Morning light was streaming through the window, and he looked around the room through half-closed eyes and rubbed his face.

"Wow, that was something else," Harry murmured to himself.

On the desk in front of him were the gifts from his trainers. As he picked up each object and read the inscriptions, a feeling of determination started to build inside his chest; he felt as if he'd been infused with gratitude and goodwill. He quickly composed an email inviting his staff to a mandatory meeting the next day, then picked up his phone and dialed a number.

"Hi, David? This is Harry Green. I haven't had the chance to properly welcome you to the team yet. Are you free for lunch on Tuesday?"

Glossary

TRIBALRY: The art of building connection and community

FIRE TRIANGLE

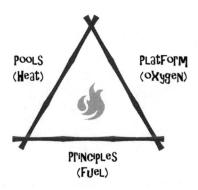

PRINCIPLES

1. Decide to Tribe

Tribe leaders teach their members how to stop being gladiators and help them become successful tribe members instead. The success of their tribe is always their primary concern.

2. Invisible Threads

Tribe leaders understand that every opportunity has its root in a relationship. "We cannot live for ourselves alone. Our lives are connected by a thousand invisible threads."

3. Avoid Relationship Arrogance

Tribe leaders don't prioritize relationships based on a forecasted return on investment, and they don't predetermine whether relationships are valuable before having meaningful interaction.

4. Just Because

Tribe leaders possess authentic motives and build relationships "just because." They recognize that every person is inherently valuable.

5. Learn, Serve, Grow

Tribe leaders apply the process of learn, serve, grow to predictably grow relationships by learning about others and serving their needs.

POOLS

Tribe leaders are committed to helping their tribes spend less time inside fast-paced, task-centered environments and more time relaxing and connecting inside the slower pace of a pool.

1. Fish Profile: Who is it for?

2. Designed Emotion: How will it make them feel?

3. Outside the Current: Is it in a non-task-centered environment?

4. Effective Pull: Is the experience compelling?

5. Connects Participants: Is there facilitated interaction?

6. Name: Does it have a memorable name?

7. Duplicatable: Can it be repeated?

PLATFORM

Tribe leaders train and motivate their tribe members to learn about and serve each other through the private, online platform, tribalry.com.

Sources

Chapter 1: Harry Green

The Godfather. Film. Directed by Francis Ford Coppola. Hollywood, CA: Paramount Pictures, 1972.

Chapter 2: Patrick O'Flannery

Dickens, Charles. *A Christmas Carol*. 1st ed. Cambridge, MA: Candlewick Press, 2006. First published December 19, 1843.

Chapter 6: Self-Made Myths

Walt Disney

Eliot, Marc. *Walt Disney: Hollywood's Dark Prince*. New York: Birch Lane Press, 1993.

Gabler, Neal. *Walt Disney: The Triumph of the American Imagination*. New York: Random House, 2006.

Estée Lauder

"Cosmetics Queen Estée Lauder Dies." BBC News. 25 April 2004. http://news.bbc.co.uk/go/fr/-/1/hi/world/americas/3658375.stm

Lauder, Estée. *Estée: A Success Story*. New York: Random House, 1985.

Larry Page and Sergey Brin

Batelle, John. *The Search: How Google and Its Rivals Rewrote the Rules of Business and Transformed Our Culture*. New York: Penguin Group, 2005.

Vise, David A. *The Google Story*. New York: Random House, 2005.

Charles Taylor

Charles "Charley" Taylor (inventor). 2011. http://www.nationalaviation.org/taylor-charles./

Thomas Edison

Caldicott, Sarah Miller. *Midnight Lunch: The 4 Phases of Team collaboration Success from Thomas Edison's Lab.* New York: John Wiley & Sons, 2012.

About the Authors

A brother-sister team, Jared Stewart and Sarah Waugh are the authors of *Tribalry: A Business Tale*. They are living proof that you can work with family and still come out friends.

Jared Stewart is the founder and CEO of Tribalry. Jared's unbounded passion for people and relationships sparked the creation of Influence International in 2000 and Tribalry in 2014. The company's intellectual property and relationship-building systems include world-class software, paradigm-shifting content and proprietary event systems which combine to significantly increase the quality and speed of the relationship-building process.

Sarah Stewart Waugh is president of the Training Division at Tribalry. She graduated from Brigham Young University with a bachelor's degree in English and received a master's degree from Northern Arizona University in education. She taught writing for five years before being approached by her brother in 2004 to help him translate the company's relationship-building culture into a fable. She currently oversees all Tribalry trainings, events, and publications.

Made in the USA
San Bernardino, CA
26 May 2017